Trapping the Elusive I

MW01078575

By Rick Crawford

Trapping the Elusive Bobcat

By
Rick Crawford

Dedicated to the memory of Eric Kuper
my friend and trapping partner.

Trapping the Elusive Bobcat

Revised Edition

First Printing Dec 2006

All photos by the author unless otherwise noted
Drawings, charts and graphs by the author unless noted

Copywrite Notice All Rights Reserved

Table of Contents

Welcome to bobcat country!

Notice tom bobcat caught under the large pinyon tree on top edge of some ledges.

The Aspen Fence

Velvet paws of daggers sheathed
Stealthily walk the wood beneath
High above the layered snow
Lightening steel in calico
Miles zigzagging hence and fro
Daunting wet and falling snow
Broken then a wooden ledge
Hesitance to breech lanes edge
Graceful glide to land beneath
Pug marks laced by passing feet

Rick Crawford 1996

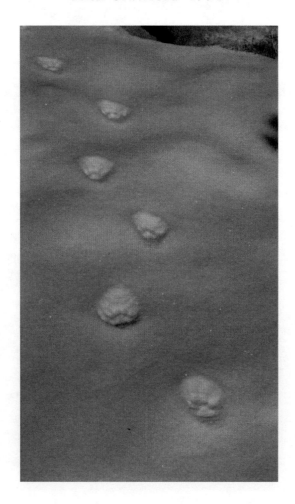

I have had a passion for Nature and wildlife from the time I escaped my mothers arms to play outside. It started with a very domestic, rural back yard chasing squirrels and sparrows with a homemade bow and arrows. It has become my path in life haunting and hunting some of North America's most rugged and remote landscapes as a professional hunting guide and trapper.

I spend over 300 days a year in the great outdoors trapping, scouting and guiding hunters. I always look forward to the time my last hunt is over and I can lay out my trap line.

I vividly recall the first bobcat I trapped as a boy. A friend and I went to check some of my fox traps before school one crisp autumn morning. After visiting a few uneventful sets, we followed a fence line through the river bottom to a trail set. The trap was gone! Drag marks left by the log drag, led us to a net fence. There we found the drag and several feet of chain, tangled in the fence. The wire I had used to attach the trap to the chain was broken. A large, strong animal had torn up the surrounding landscape and escaped with my trap still on its foot!

Much to our mothers distress, and the ire of the school principal, we spent the better part of a school day searching for and tracking my catch. Occasionally, we found scratch marks in the hard clay soil where the animal had put its foot down to rest or drag the trap.

After several hundred yards of difficult tracking we found where the animal had entered a sandy wash bottom. There things became a maze of confusion. Animal tracks and drag marks went up and down the wash several times as the creature considered an escape route. At this point my friend and I split up each going in the opposite direction. As I followed the maze of tracks the signs began to diminish, until eventually one set continued up the wash, then turned up a smaller side wash. Twenty feet into this drainage it made a sharp turn to the left. I had my head down, intent on the sign when some intuition made the hair stand up on my neck. Almost at the same instant, I realized the small wash was a dead end. A washout had been created in the hard clay formation where water poured in from above during a rain storm, run off or a flash flood.

Standing at the bottom of the washout, I followed the the scratch marks going up the wall. My skin began to crawl, as by some primeval sense I felt eyes burning into my skull. Slowly, I looked up and right into the eyes of a very agitated, very large, bobcat. He sat crouched on a shelf four feet above my head! As I kept my eyes on him and slowly brought up the .22 rim fire rifle I carried, the cat opened its mouth to show a set of large, formidable canine teeth and let out a savage growl. Pumped with a burst of adrenaline and a sudden instinct for survival, I quickly raised the gun and fired, hitting the cat just above its left eye. Leaping straight into the air, it tumbled right on top of me! Wildly flailing my arms like a school girl trying to fight, I threw the cat off. Thankfully it was dead before it hit the ground, although its still twitching muscles and nerves kept me thrilled for a few exhilarating seconds!

A short few minutes later my friend came running to see what the shooting was about. We were both excited about my catch and the big, beautifully furred bobcat.

Such a dramatic, exciting experience early in my life, and the praise and money the fur brought from the fur buyer, started me on a path of lifelong passion for trapping and studying these tough, beautiful felines.

Over the next few years as I studied bobcats and their habits I began to catch them in numbers. I read everything I could find about trapping and about bobcats and managed to find two books that talked about trapping them. One was by O.L. Butcher, a booklet, titled "Professional Cat Trapping" There was also a chapter in S. Stanley Hawbaker's book, "Trapping North American Furbearers" under "Trapping the Wild Cat." Eight pages of pretty much the same sets and information as the booklet by O. L. Butcher. At the time, of Hawbaker and Butcher, most trappers only trapped bobcats for bounty. It wasn't until years later that bobcat fur came into fashion, and the price of

bobcat pelts made trappers take notice. During the early 1970's the fur market was going strong. At the time I started trapping in 1978, bobcat fur was on a downward tick, but still worth trapping. I could make $300 for a XL, Prime, A Grade, bobcat termed, Lynx Cat for my region. Averages prime bobcats were around $170. During the early 80's the market for bobcats started going back up and trappers all over the country started trapping cats again. About this time many states set low limits, that made it impossible to focus on just bobcats. It also kept demand for their fur high, until the stock market crash in 1987.

Since this time, the market ebb and flow, and foreign demand for this beautiful fur, have anchored bobcats as a top seller in the fur trade and kept me chasing them out of intrigue and financial necessity. Between, Mother Nature and the stock market, my seasonal business has often felt more like a chess match than a profitable business. Now, 38 years later, I am still trapping bobcats, and enjoy it as much as I did as a boy. Trap checking time is still like Christmas as I look forward to the presents left in my traps!

The elusive bobcat is found in nearly every state and providence on the North American Continent. They are found north to Canada where they overlap habitat with the lynx and as far south as Mexico. A bobcat's home range can vary greatly. From less than one square mile to 40 square miles or more. Finding bobcats can be easy or difficult, depending on habitat type and population density. The availability of prey species, and the population of larger predators that

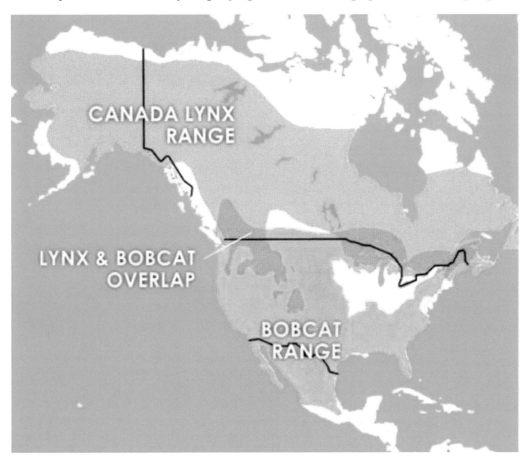

prey on bobcats affects their range and distribution. The amount, density and distribution of vegetation and cover, where a bobcat can stalk prey and hide from larger predators, including; man, coyotes, mountain lions and large birds of prey, are key factors in their distribution.

Many bobcat studies have indicated that bobcats need areas of rough overgrown vegetation, such as forests, swamps, river bottoms mountains, deserts and wilderness to survive in good numbers. Areas that contain a variety of features, such as ponds, streams, lakes, caves, rocky outcroppings, boulder fields, gulleys, ravines, and wash bottoms in addition to the rough, overgrown vegetation will be outstanding bobcat habitat.

Rural farming areas can hold good numbers of bobcats providing there are rough tracks of undeveloped land near the farming areas where bobcats can retreat during the day to rest without being disturbed.

Bobcats need areas of rough habitat that have avoided the encroach of civilization, they need an ample prey base, water and safety from larger predators.

In the more open plains, bobcats will survive in the bluffs, rocks and river bottoms. In the East, look for them in the swamps, river bottoms, and forests. In the West they can be found in the deserts, mountains, river bottoms, and rim-rock country. In the South, where they are the most numerous they inhabitant the vast brush lands, river bottoms, forests and lake regions. In the North they prefer the lower foothills, river bottoms, lakes and forests.

The key to finding bobcats in all of these habitat types is to find areas where the ecotones meet and overlap.

Pine forest ecotone

From Wikipedia: "An **ecotone** is a transition area between two biomes. It is where two communities meet and integrate. It may be narrow or wide, and it may be local (the zone between a field and forest) or regional (the transition between forest and grassland ecosystems). An ecotone may appear on the ground as a gradual blending of the two communities across a broad area, or it may manifest itself as a sharp boundary line.

The word ecotone was coined from a combination of eco(logy) plus tone from the Greek tonos, or tension. In other words, a place where ecologies are in tension.

There are several distinguishing features of an ecotone. First, an ecotone can have a sharp vegetation transition, with a distinct line between two communities. For example, a change in colors of grasses or plant life can indicate an ecotone. Second, a change in physiognomy, (physical appearance of plant species) can be an indicator. Scientists look at color variations and changes in plant height. Third, a change of species can signal an ecotone. There will be specific organisms on one side of an ecotone or the other.

Ecotone edge along an old alfalfa field and and a tree line.

Other factors can illustrate or obscure an ecotone, for example, migration and the establishment of new plants. These are known as spatial mass effects, which are noticeable because some organisms will not be able to form self-sustaining populations if they cross the ecotone. If different species can survive in both communities of the tow biomes, then the ecotone is considered to have, species richness; biologists measure this when studying the food chain and success of organisms. Lastly, the abundance of exotic species in an ecotone can reveal the type of biome or efficiency of the two communities sharing space. Because an ecotone is the zone in which two communities integrate, many different forms of life have to live together and compete for space. Therefore, an ecotone can create a diverse ecosystem." End Quote

From this we can understand that at ecotone borders or areas where habitat and species overlap will hold the most food sources, prey species, water, and cover. These areas will be the place where most bobcats and other furbearing animals will live, reproduce and survive.

Bobcats behave much like any other cat, climbing, scratching, yowling and hunting. They are by nature curious but have unique habits. They can be aloof and lazy if the mood suits them or excessively inquisitive as indicated by the quote, "Curiosity killed the cat"! It is the trappers job to bring out this curiosity by appealing to its senses of sight, smell, territory, prey drive and sex drive. We will go into detail about the things that can be done to accomplish this later in the book as we talk about setting traps.

Bobcats can live near towns, rural areas and farming communities, providing prey is abundant and hiding cover available. For the most part however, cats prefer rugged, brushy, lonely country with lots of space to explore and hunt. In the East and South they prefer large tracts of wooded areas, waterways, swamps and bottom land and brushy country. In the Midwest they prefer lowland water ways, crop lands with adjacent tracks of wooded land, higher badlands and breaks country. Large crop fields with mice and rabbits and undeveloped areas are places to check for bobcats. In Western mountain

regions they wander wooded trails and back roads, stream sides, lakes, rock piles and out croppings. They will haunt beaver ponds and rabbit lairs in every habitat type. In the Desert Southwest, bobcats are found in canyons, dry riverbeds and around rim rock, craggy cliffs and projecting mesas. They like pinyon/juniper country that meets the sagebrush and scrub oak patches. They like the areas where the lower pinyon and juniper gives way to higher ponderosa pines, scrub oak hillsides and openings in the forest. They will be found around desert waterways, lava patches, canyons and cacti forests. Look for bobcats in the roughest areas with the least access and you will be well on your way to finding a good population of cats to trap.

Like all members of the cat family, bobcats are **nocturnal (most active at night)** or more accurately **diurnal** (most active at dusk and dawn). Their large keen eyes absorb a lot of light to give them super night vision. They can detect the smallest movement of a mouse. They also have amazing hearing. Their large ears with the sensitive tufts on the tip can sense sound vibrations much to small for human ears. A bobcats sense of smell is not as well developed as predators of the canine family, but is still very acute, and can determine the marks and signs left by other bobcats and predators.

Bobcats have large, soft padded feet like furry slippers with four razor sharp retractable claws, which they use to catch and hold prey, defend themselves and climb. They are excellent climbers and like to lay in the sun on the fork of large trees.

Bobcats are arguably the best camouflaged predators in North America. With their ultra soft fur and light spotted belly which reflects light back onto shadows, effectively softening them, and the darker browns, grays with camouflaged black spots, that absorb sunlight and resists reflection. When we add to these features, large, formidable canine teeth, uncanny stealth, agility and lightening spurts of speed, punctuated with amazing leaps, we reveal a nightmare to rabbits and small game!

Bobcats have prominent tufted ears, large brown-green eyes, tufted cheek hairs and a short three to six inch tail marked with two or more black bars and a black tip.

Their fur is fine and silky with various tones of gray, black, blue, reddish-brown, marked with black spots or rosettes. Their belly fur is white or off-white to light brown, with various marking of more black spots.

Bobcats range in size from 15 to 40 pounds with the occasional larger or smaller specimen. Males are typically larger and better marked than females. Bobcats stand from 16 to 18 inches at the shoulder and range from 29 to 45 inches in length.

Rabbits, rats, mice, squirrels and birds make up the majority of a bobcats diet. Other prey species include deer, pronghorn antelope, foxes and other smaller predators, beaver, raccoon,skunks, porcupines, bats, lizards, insects, snakes, fish and other small domestic animals that they encounter in their wanderings. Bobcats will eat a small amount of vegetation and fruit matter as season and instinct provides, but are mainly carnivorous.

Bobcats prefer to catch and eat their own prey but a road killed deer, or winter killed game will suit them if it is fresh and they are hungry. They will eat rotten or tainted meat only if very hungry or starving.

Bobcats are good hunters and have a large menu but females have a tough job of rearing young and the males wander far and wide overlapping the range of several breeding females, and must fight and protect their range from other encroaching males. These factors, along with the extremes of weather, drought and other competing predators, rabbit and rodent cycles and nature in general, keeps bobcats strong and healthy by keeping them fit and hungry.

Canadian Lynx: Stock Photo

Historically bobcat territory overlapped that of its close cousin, the lynx in the intermountain west and northeast. Now, this overlapping of habitat occurs mainly at the borders of the US and Canada as shown by the distribution map on a previous page.

The lynx is shown to be a more sensitive species and is more shy and reclusive. It has fewer litters, and is more dependent on rabbit populations and cycles than bobcats are. The lynx prefers colder climates, higher elevations, and more timbered country. Slightly larger than the bobcat, lynx have huge, furry feet, custom tailored for moving over snow-covered terrain in search of their favorite prey, the snowshoe hare. Unlike the bobcat, the lynx is now listed as a threatened species in every state and region except Alaska and Canada, and cannot be hunted and trapped outside these regions.

Bobcats mate in the early spring, from mid February to early April. Breeding time is affected by longitude and latitude as well as weather conditions and elevation. Females that are not bred in the spring may cycle again, and breed later. The females gestation period is approximately 65 days, and average litter size is three kittens.

Snowshoe Hare

Bobcat kittens are quite hearty and providing the mother has an adequate food supply, they do well and develop quickly. At ten days, they open their eyes and begin developing their extraordinary coordination. Kittens nurse for two months, then begin following their mother on hunting forays. If conditions are good, the mother may allow the young bobcats to stay with her the first winter.

Females cats mature faster than the males and can breed their first year. Male bobcats are larger but not sexually mature until their second year.

Bobcats are very strong for their size and can and do kill domestic livestock, sheep, goats, poultry and pets. They can take down a full sized deer. When they are finished with a meal, they will cover the remains with grass, sticks and dirt to hide it from birds and other predators. They will return to feed on larger kills until it is gone or starts to get rotten.

COVERT   09.23.2015 22:23:28   ⟲11 013°C 055°F ▥9

Cats can be finicky. They can seem indifferent or aloof. Sometimes it takes quite an effort to get a bobcat's attention. If you do not understand their nature and what makes them tick, trapping them can be frustrating! Many times when I first started trapping bobcats I had them walk just feet away from what I considered to be the perfect set. To begin to understand some of this behavior just watch a house cat. The harder you try to get a house cat to come to you, the more they avoid you. Ignore them, and they will often become a pest! A cat with a full belly and something else on its mind will lay around in the sun and ignore pretty much everything except for keeping one eye open watching the dog! Cats just do the things that suit them at the time and for the mood they are in. Things that move, make enticing sounds, smell irresistible or arouse their territorial instincts will be investigated by bobcats, providing they are hungry or in the right mood. The attraction must also be close enough to the cat that they feel like responding. Because of this, it is critical that bobcat traps and sets are as close to their natural travel routes and hunting areas as possible.

Bobcats do have habits that make them predictable, in spite of their fussy natures. They must hunt, eat, drink, avoid larger predators, and follow their sex drive and territorial survival instincts. By making sets in the areas that naturally appeal to these needs and habits, you will, with a little patience, catch bobcats. As an example I want to point out a few things. Make bait sets and flag sets in areas bobcats hunt. Use their territorial instinct against them at scratch up sets and tree markings. Use their sex drive against them at a toilet set, and in between these places use curiosity against them with a flat set with bones or a large bait. Think about this last paragraph and I think you will figure it out how to catch a bobcat.

Bobcats have a fairly regular agenda. They follow the same paths and routes along travel corridors as they move through their home range. They snoop in favorite caves and holes where they have caught mice and pack rats before. They visit rabbit thickets and places where ground birds live and roost. They have toilet spots and territorial markers where they scratch, urinate and poop. Bobcat feces resemble small link sausages. These droppings are usually 3-5 inches long and ¾ inch in diameter. These droppings will contain fur, feathers, bone fragments and digested meat. They will be free of the berries and seeds of fox and coyote scat.

A good bobcat toilet location can be one of the best bobcat sets there is. Bobcats will visit a toilet on their regular rounds to use it or see if anyone else they know has. Because of this a toilet is both a territorial location and a location to check up on the opposite sex. Do not destroy or reconstruct a bobcat toilet. When you make a set at a toilet location use a drag or cable slide set to move the trapped animal away from the set without damaging it. If you do this, a good toilet location will last for many years. I will show details of these sets in the chapter on Bobcat Trapping Sets.

A good way to peer into a bobcats habits and personality, is to follow fresh bobcat tracks in the snow. You will see that a cat may just as soon walk along from tree to tree, crawling under low limbs and following tight little drainage's, as walk an open lane or trail. Cats will often cross roads through culverts, and use logs to cross a stream they can't easily jump across. Bobcats can swim and will if they can't avoid it, but they prefer to stay dry particularly during cold weather.

Bobcats have a habit of walking under cliff edges and overhanging vegetation to stay out of the snow, or rain. Once I followed cat tracks that walked the top of an aspen rail fence for over a mile to stay out of the snow. I could see occasional foot prints where snow stuck to the fence and the bobcat could not avoid it. When the fence ended at a gate opening the cat jumped down crossed the opening and jumped back up on top of the almost-dry top rail and continued on its way. This incident inspired the poem at the beginning of the book, "The Aspen Fence".

Bobcats in a hurry may travel lanes, trails and road edges, providing there is cover near by. If they are hunting they will prowl slowly just inside the brush line, peering out, every sense alert! Bobcats love sandy beach areas and soft, fine sediment deposits below ledges. It is such places they often choose for their toilet locations. They like these locations just like a house cat likes little Johnny's sand box to take a dump! The digging is easy and sand feels great under their toes!

Bobcats like to travel field edges, fence lines, old irrigation ditches and crop windrows while they hunt and sneak around. Beaver houses and dams are favorite places for a bobcat to prowl looking for a meal or investigating the pungent smell of a caster mound left by the resident beaver.

In rocky canyons, bobcats walk the bottoms of cliff edges and along the very top edge of the ledge or top. They will follow ridge lines, cross through saddles and follow game trails up and down the mountains and cliffs to hunting areas and water, then back into the higher country to lay in the sun or survey their domain.

Bobcats frequent distinctive terrain features or rock formations that stand out. They will often make toilets around these features. Prominent trees with a large overhanging canopy and soft loose duff or dirt beneath are also favorite places for a toilet location. If the tree is prominent and unique, if it stands out to you, it will stand out to a bobcat and could be a favorite haunt.

In areas where large trees are scarce or rock formations infrequent, any such feature could be a real attraction to any bobcats in the area. Any feature or location that stands out to you will stand out to bobcats and could attract them. Old abandoned cabins, sawmill slash piles, strange rock formations, caves, large dead trees, old dump sites or abandoned vehicles that provide shelter for small rodents and rabbits will be prime bobcat attractions.

You must spend time in the field finding bobcat sign and getting to know the country and animals you trap. No amount of book information can replace this hands on insight you must gain if you are to become a successful trapper. You must get a **feel** for bobcats, and learn the features and areas they like to frequent in your area. Remember to record your findings and observations in a notebook to job your memory and use as a trap placement guide.

A bobcat's habitat area which I will refer to as its home range, can vary greatly in size, depending on many factors. Studies by wildlife biologists and graduate students show these great variances. Home ranges have been shown to be as small as 5/8 of a mile and as large as 42 square miles. The female bobcat's home range is usually quite a bit smaller than that of the male. Typically the larger tom's range includes the range of several female cats. Beyond the breeding season, males and females grudgingly tolerate each other; but mature females usually don't tolerate other mature females close to their favorite areas. Some exceptions seem to be shown to direct offspring that has taken up residence near by; but if times get tough the old female will run off the less dominate cats.

Very nice blue phase bobcat

In one trapping area, I caught five bobcats. Four females and one huge tom. I turned the three young females loose and kept the tom, one old scarred up female that showed no signs of kittens and another big female that didn't have teats showing and was a beautiful, dark blue color.

Since that time this great habitat area has exploded with bobcats that the old timers had been keeping at bay. Now the area holds twice as many cats and I routinely catch two or three males and an an older female beyond breeding years. I turn all the younger bobcats loose. If I can see a female has worn down teeth and no teats showing, it is time to harvest the cat and open the area up for younger breeding animals. A wise trapper can manage his trap line to produce more animals by selective harvest and rotation of trapping areas. As with any species, their home range is determined by food and water sources. If prey is abundant and water readily available a bobcat's home range will be quite small. More animals will be available for the trapper and less work will be involved in locating and catching them.

Mature males are far less tolerant of each other than the females and will fight when they meet. As with any species individuals differ as much as instinct, personality, and survival will allow. Bobcat relations is a rather complex and interlocking puzzle. Trying to completely figure them and their dynamics out is impossible. The trapper should learn as much as he can, but success will come by following the basics of finding good habitat with plenty of game, water and cover. Then concentrating on finding bobcat sign, toilet locations and travel routes.

Bobcats, particularly the tom cats, scratch the ground and tree trunks to mark their territory. They also make small mounds of dirt leaves and grass called a scratch up that they urinate on to mark their territory. The males will back up and spray urine and in the process you will occasionally catch one by a back foot at a scent post or scratch up set.

During the breeding season of late January to March I make many double bobcat sets. This ensures if I catch a female I will often catch a male too. Since I am focusing on the larger toms and want to keep the breeding females around, I turn the females loose. Once you have had some experience with bobcats you will be able to tell the females apart from the males. Females have smaller bodies, heads and less distinctive cheek ruffs. The males testicles are visible under their tail. If there is any question you can use your dispatch, choke stick to look them over. Make sure they are well caught before you get inquisitive or you might get a surprise!

All bobcats should be dispatched with a choke stick also called an animal handler stick. Because of their anatomy you can quickly shut off a bobcats blood supply to its brain with a choke stick and they will pass out within a few seconds and die in a minute or less. Because of this when releasing a young cat or female, you must move quickly once a bobcat passes out. Get the cat out of the trap, push it away from you and quickly remove the stick and step back 20 feet until the bobcat has regained consciousness and slipped away. Do not stand next to a released cat or it will almost assuredly jump on you and take a quick bite. The animal must get its wits and realize it is free and move away on its own, or it may still consider its self still in the trap.

If you choose to harvest a bobcat, take your time releasing it from the trap until you are sure it is dead. I wait two minutes after it is unconscious then leave the choke stick locked firmly in place while I reset the trap. I know guys that have lost a choke stick and or an animal by taking the stick off too soon, or using a chock stick that does not have a locking device which allows the noose to relax and animal to regain unconsciousness. I am sure you can imagine the confusion and disappointment from losing a big  bobcat or both a bobcat and your dispatch stick! To sum up this chapter, home range and habitat can vary greatly, depending upon the availability of food, shelter and water sources. Better habitat will contain several types of prey species in good numbers, good cover and ample water sources. With this type of habitat, a female bobcat can have a small home range. Several other females can live near by in harmony, and the males will be around to keep track of the females. Good habitat allows more cats to exist in a smaller area. This results in less leg work and faster catches for the trapper. When you consider everything that goes into trapping, time, fuel cost and hard work, it really pays off to find good cat habitat.

Finding Bobcats

When I go into the field to look for good bobcat habitat, I first look for bobcat sign. I look for tracks, scat and scratch posts.

Bobcat scat, are 4-6" long droppings with distinctive segments. They are usually easy to identify because of their segmented characteristics and lack of seeds and vegetable matter that is found in coyote and fox droppings. Cat droppings will contain fur, bone fragments, feathers and digested meat.

A bobcat attempts to bury its droppings but just as a house cat does not always do a good job of getting things covered up. At a well used toilet location in fine or sandy soil you will see droppings of different ages. From dark fresh ones to older faded and even white ones. As the cat attempt to bury a fresh turd, it often uncovers an older one, and a toilet that has been used for several years will show many droppings.

I look for tracks in the sandy areas along the shores of lakes and streams or under overhanging rocks. I look for pinch points and places where every animal in an area must travel to get from point A to point B. The rims and bottoms of small canyons and swamps or gulleys that provide obstacles that force every critter to go a certain way around are great places to look for tracks or toilet locations. Large trees that stand out, or smaller ones that are conveiently located at trail junctions, or along rims or field edges are good places to look for droppings or tracks. Scratch marks on the trees bark, or scratched up dirt near their bases can indicate bobcat activity and are excellent locations for a trap.

The second thing I look for scouting for bobcats are signs of abundant prey species. Not only is this fairly easy to determine, it is the biggest factor in finding cats. I search for rabbit tracks and dropping. Pack rat nests and muskrat houses. I look for signs of ground birds like turkeys, chucker and quail. Marsh lands with pheasants and ducks and shore birds are great places to look. A key sign of a good area, can be be numerous dead rabbits along the road ways. If it is good habitat with lots of prey, there will also be other predators like fox, coyote and badger in the area that will help pay your expenses and make trapping more interesting. On the flip side too many coyotes or the presence of mountain lions or wolves will really put a damper on your bobcat efforts so you must take these things into consideration as you scout. If an area has numerous coyotes then make a big effort for them, thin them out to pay your expenses as well as open up habitat for the bobcats that are around.

Wetlands hold many bobcats.

With a little experience a trapper can easily tell the difference between fox, coyote, bobcat and domestic dogs and house cat tracks.

Abundant game in good bobcat habitat usually means a population of bobcats, unless some factor is keeping their numbers low. Some factors that could cause this is too much trapping and hunting pressure. Low numbers of bobcats could also be attributed to an over abundance of coyotes and mountain lions.

Mountain lions like the same terrain and habitat types as bobcats. They usually fill a different niche in nature, feeding on larger prey such as deer, young elk and turkeys. Lions normally have a much larger territory than bobcats, and a smaller population base. Bobcats can usually live quite well by avoiding the larger cats when they pass through their hunting grounds, and by living in smaller pockets not frequented by lions, which are usually hunting larger game. However, when bobcats and mountain lions are

Mountain lion investigating bobcat set

pushed together for various reasons like heavy snow, a limited prey base, or encroaching human population, a lion will kill and eat any bobcat it can catch, and be happy doing it!

Areas that develop a numerous population of lions will cause the same effect, as young lions start preying on smaller predators and prey in an attempt to compete and survive.

A large population of coyotes in an area can have the same effect as a population of mountain lions. Coyotes eat up the prey base, harass mature bobcats and kill young cats caught out in the open. Bobcats will not tolerate too many encounters with aggressive coyotes and will pack up and move out of an area. In a one on one encounter, a mature bobcat has little to fear from a coyote, but when coyotes are hunting in groups or become aggressive because of limited food sources, it causes a bobcat to alter their behavior and makes it difficult for them to hunt, relax and feel safe. The good news is

that there is a remedy for a coyote problem. It is fixed by setting a bunch of traps targeting these yodel dogs! A good coyote trapper can put a real dent in a coyote population and put a lot of money in his wallet.

Where To Set Your Bobcat Traps

Bobcats have their own unique habits and ways they move through their home range. You can catch dozens of coyotes and foxes in an area that contains bobcats and seldom catch a single bobcat if you do not understand how they hunt and travel through their habitat.

Coyotes and red foxes hunt the outside edge of fields and openings, while a bobcat will prefer to remain along the inside edge of the cover. A trap set in a harvested crop field, 15 feet off the edge of a brushy point, will product red fox and coyote, but seldom a bobcat. A trap set right on the edge of the brush line, or even better, in some small opening just inside it, will, over time, produce every bobcat hunting the area. I might also add you will catch more gray

fox, raccoon and skunk in the bobcat set as well.

Bobcats like to travel up against the edge of things. They prefer to move through cover and stay hidden. Because of this trait and their exceptional camouflage, humans seldom see a bobcat in the wild.

Bobcats travel and hunt up and down the terrain keeping to cover. Canines travel openings and trails and hunt along the terrain. Bobcats are hunting for a living and must locate, stalk and catch prey almost every day. This takes patience and cautious movement. They must always be cautious and alert, ready to freeze at a moments notice and then carefully plan each stalk. Canines on

21

the other hand are the proverbial hunter-gatherers. They eat 50% or less fresh meat and the rest is carrion, vegetable and fruit matter they gather/locate. This is why a coyote moves across and area using its nose to check the rising or falling wind currents and thermals, he is using his nose to find kills left by other animals, or ripened food sources, as well as hunting small animals. A coyote does not need to be as cautious as a bobcat while hunting small game. They have the ability to flush-out and run-down prey with great endurance, while a bobcat is dependent on getting close then making a lightening strike on small game or birds.

Mule Deer killed by coyotes

Bobcats love rocks or all shapes and sizes, and will hunt up and down and through them looking for mice, rats and rabbits. In their travels they encounter the edge line of ledges and eventually the top of the ledge, mesa or plateau. Because most rock formations have these top, middle and bottom structure lines that can be seen looking at them from a distance or on Google Earth, these make excellent travel lanes for bobcats. These features also become a barrier that a bobcat must move along until he can find a way up or down. With a little effort, excellent trap locations can be found where bobcats and other traveling critters are funneled predictably through or along these narrow areas. Spots like this are a gold mine to the trapper!

It takes hard work and effort to climb around the rocks and along rock walls and ledges, but it will be worth your efforts if there are bobcats in the area. These activities will keep you in shape! You will find bobcat toilets, pack rat nests, overhanging rocks and caves that make excellent, weather-proof set locations and pinch points where bobcats come and go. With a little experience you will soon be able to stand back and look at a rock formation or feature and predict the places you can find bobcat sign and make good sets.

To start this search, check the very bottom edge of any formation or outcropping. Check the ends or turning points of formations. Look for game trails that go up or across. Check saddles and passes and check the highest point and the ledges beneath the highest point. Look at any interesting or stand-out features and formations. Caves and overhanging ledges or hanging gardens where water seeps fromthe rock and lush vegetation grows, are some good features to look for. Any time you find a bobcat track or dropping take note of it and follow its line of travel looking for a good spot to set a trap.

A good water source below a series of dry ledges is an excellent opportunity to catch bobcats and other predators when they come to water. Traps set along trails and near any water source in desert country can be a gold mine for the bobcat trapper. Every remote water location in dry country are worth checking for signs of bobcats.

Trapping in rock and ledge country is hard work and you have to have a lot of confidence in your trapping ability and know bobcats are in the area to hike around in the ledges with traps and gear on your back. If the cats are there, however, ledges can be golden. Most other bobcat trappers will not trap in the ledges even if they know cats are there. It is just too damn hard for most beer drinking, couch potato, wanna-be trappers to go there!

There is one great bobcat trapping area that a lot of trappers in one of location I trap, frequent. They drive down a canyon road and make sets along the dry washes and bases of the bottom ledges. They do catch a few cats now and again, but while they are doing this, I drive along with a pair of binoculars checking my sets along the top edges and the trails that lead up and down and all places in between. I always catch more bobcats than all the other trappers combined. I catch the largest toms, I catch the cats before they have a chance to descend and find the other trapper's traps at the bottom!

One day, I was talking to an old trapper that considers himself the best trapper in the country. He was bragging about all his experiences and knowledge of bobcat habits. After explaining to me how bobcats only go into the ledges after a big snow, he asked me why he always saw me climbing around in the a fore mentioned canyon while the weather was good. I just smiled and said I like to explore. I do like to hike and explore but the real reason he saw my truck parked and me climbing was to gather up another bobcat that was stuck in one of my traps!

I always try to wait until passers-by are gone, before I retrieve critters from my traps. It is better for business and keeping my trap locations secret and helps avoid the issue of theft. I think it was Russ Carman in his excellent book, **Foxes By The 100's** , that quoted an old trapper who said, "Don't advertise, unless you have something to sell"!

Another good reason to trap around ledges, is the the very structure of the terrain forces certain travel routes. Learn to read and set these routes and it is not hard at all. Once a bobcat leaves the confines of the ledge country, then he becomes less predictable!

A great example of distinct topo lines where bobcats will travel and good set spots marked X

Earlier, I mentioned that I drive along and check my traps that are set on the tops and up in the ledges with my binoculars. That wasn't a typo. I make my sets using trap indicators to tell me when I have a trapped bobcat. When these indicators are used properly, even a small animal will trip the indicator and tell you it is time to climb the hill and retrieve your catch.

It is quick and easy to drive along and stop at landmarks and check sets with indicator flags. The way I make these indicators is with bright or contrasting colors of surveyors tape and some wire or heavy fishing line. While I am making my sets, I attach a length of light wire or heavy gage fishing line to a section of trap chain about 6 inches from the trap itself. I blend this wire or line into my set, so that it is hard to see then run it up the face of the rock, or up to a branch of a likely tree. With a nail wedged into a crack in the rock or a bit of wire tied to a small dead twig, I tie my flag so the wind won't blow it down, but the pull of a trapped animal will.

Another way you can do this is by putting a section of the surveyors flagging under a couple pound rock and letting the rest with your wire attached hang down. You must make sure the flag is visible from below when you know where to look with your binoculars.

Sometimes I will use a long stick leaned up with part of the trap chain wrapped around the base it so it will fall over when a catch is made. What ever you devise, that will reliably indicate when a catch is made will work. The object is to save time, money and effort.

Flagged indicator set with ringtail cat and Another flagged set still ready for a bobcat

When I make sets up in the rocks and ledges I nearly always make two sets at every location. Rats, rabbits, spotted skunks, gray fox and ringtail cats, will often get caught in your bobcat traps. If this happens you will still have a trap available to catch a bobcat if he comes along shortly after the first animal is caught. Often the trapped animal will bring in a curious cat who gets caught investigating or eats the other trapped critter then gets caught snooping around after its meal, looking for dessert!

I don't want anyone to get the idea that bobcats can only be found in or around ledges or this is the only place to trap them. This isn't true at all. Bobcats are just quite predictable in ledge country, and they are easy to find and catch where rocky ledge country is found. In the absence of rock formations or ledges, bobcats become less predictable and the trapper must discover the areas the bobcats are using and catch them there.

Finding sign is the only sure way to determine if a bobcat is using any area. Game trails are a favorite haunt of the bobcat for obvious reasons! It is a good area to run into groceries! You must look closely to find bobcat tracks. They have very soft, furry, feet and their tracks can be difficult to see amid other tracks and sign. Melted out in the snow they can look like fox or coyote tracks.

Another great place to find bobcat tracks or droppings is along the shoulders or edges of two-track or old logging roads. Bobcats will follow these roads and openings as they travel and hunt. Rabbits and rodents like using these roads at night to feed along the edges at night and frolic with their friends. When you are driving these roads you can do a lot of scouting going slowly and watching for tracks and droppings and investigating likely looking rock piles, culverts and bridges the road goes across. Bobcats will go through dry culverts and under bridges. Both of these places

can be good locations for bobcat sets or to find tracks. Bobcats will also cross over on bridges to get to the other side of a river or creek, so the dusty sides of a dirt or gravel road are also good places to look for bobcat tracks.

Bobcats being what they are, elusive and territorial, I seldom set traps without first finding good signs of their presence. If I see a likely looking spot and have extra traps, I may gamble and put in a few sets. If it is an excellent general trap location, such as a pinch point, trail junction or some beaver lodges, you will catch coyotes and foxes anyway, so the gamble will be worth the effort.

To be a successful and efficient bobcat trapper, you should have every trap set mentally before the season ever opens. You should have two or three locations for every trap and locations you can move to after you have trapped an area over. On my lines, I am constantly scouting with ever spare moment of time. Looking for great locations, new hot spots, or check back on areas that I have successfully trapped in the past. I know of hundreds of good locations, many of which I have scouted up but never trapped yet.

26

When you have caught a number of animals and things start to slow down on your line, it may be time to move tour traps to new locations. Never try to trap all the bobcats from an area. One way you can ensure this does not happen is to turn lose most of the female bobcats you catch. I keep every medium and mature tom cat and try to remove the old females, the ones with scars, missing teeth, or that look like they are beyond kitten bearing years or ones that look barren. A mature female that shows no signs of developed tits is a good cat to remove from the ecosystem. I also release small toms that are kittens of the year. The exception to my release rule is catching a female with an obvious poor pelt genetics or health issues. A bobcat with a very

narrow strip of white on its belly or none at all, or a really red colored cat are good prospects for harvest on my trap line. I am managing for a wide white spotted belly and blue-gray back with distinctive spots. Over the years I have seen good things come from my management practices! A few sacrifices now can really pay off later. Of course all these good intentions and management will go out the window if there are other bobcat trappers in the area that don't share your views and long term approach. Because of this I try to trap areas that I have all to myself, and avoid advertising the areas I trap. If your lucky enough to find a really good area with an over abundance of bobcats, don't be afraid to keep many of the females you catch.

I like to make between 5 and 15 trap sets in a good bobcat core area or home range that I have determined holds several females and one or two toms. It takes a little experience to make an semi-educated guess what this area might be. Land formations and natural barriers like large lakes, freeways, big rivers, changing terrain, and significant elevation changes can help you make these decisions based also on your scouting efforts to locate tracks and sign.

Once you break these locations down and work out your own trap-checking routes and game laws in your area that define the required trap checking time limits, you will have a pretty good idea how to best check traps and how many traps you can run and check each day.

When you find features and locations that hold bobcats in your area, you can look at similar areas and land formations to duplicate your success in other areas.

If you find quite a lot of sign in an area, 10 to 20 bobcat sets and 10 to 20 back up sets for other predators may be a good start. I try to set high, low and on the ends of the habitat and make sets where the most sign is located. I try to catch the bobcats available, quickly and then pull my traps and move on to other areas.

Don't make 60 sets to catch 3 bobcats in one area, rather set 5 to 10 sets in 5 to 10 different bobcat home ranges to catch 10-20 bobcats, then move your traps to other areas. If you trap two or three cats from each area and move on, you will leave seed and catch the cream of the crop and move on to fresh cream. Your season catch will be larger and you will become a better trapper.

In some areas it may be difficult to take 20 cats in a season, in other areas a hard working trapper that knows bobcats can take 100 + bobcats in a season. Of course some states limit the number of bobcats you can catch. Because I live in an area that has an unlimited quota this is not an issue for me. It really boils down to where you are trapping, whether you trap where you live or travel to trap where there are good numbers of bobcats.

If you can get permission to trap private property, or find some way to access some remote areas, by four wheeler, horse back or boat, these efforts can pay off big in some great bobcat catches!

Mountain country is more difficult to trap than lower desert, canyon and ledge country. Soil types make it harder to find tracks, mountains seem to blend together and distinctive terrain features seem to blend together and be less noticeable.

In this situation I find it helpful to look at topo maps or Google Earth to locate streams, lakes, saddles, prominent peaks and the road systems and water ways. Pay attention to south-facing slopes and any distinctive features on these slopes because most of your winter trapping will be conducted here.

Mountain trapping can be more difficult a lot of good habitat to look over for key locations.

In some areas, like the regions I trap, I can trap the higher elevations during the early season, and then when winter and snow arrives I move my traps and trapping efforts to lower country. Some mild years I focus my efforts in the foot hills and higher mountain all season long. Other years I find myself miles south in the desert and rim rock country trapping a lesser quality cat but with far better results for my efforts than tramping around in knee deep snow and mud!

If you are consigned to trapping mountain country all season long, then take heart! There are things you can do to make bobcat trapping work. If you can locate wintering game areas which are usually located on lower, south-facing slopes, you can find concentrations of prey species and predators. Often great

Old kill from big game wintering range.

concentrations of animals will be living in small isolated pockets. The animals are there to escape deep snow and find grass and forage to survive. The predators are there to stay out of deep snow and feed on the prey species available

By scouting the area prior to snow fall you will locate old deer and elk droppings, bones left from winter kill and predator kills. This will tell you the areas that the prey species use for their wintering grounds. Here you can find the trees and rocks that offer weather proof trap sets and you can place your cubbys or construct them on the spot, and plan trap locations.

My friend Jared Woolsey and a couple of late season bobcats.

In some areas you may need a snowmobile or four wheeler with tracks to access your trapping area, once snow falls.

Bobcat Trapping Sets

We have finally arrived at the core subject of this book! The trapping sets that are used to catch bobcats! First I want to talk about the basics of trap setting, the tools involved in setting traps and my trap anchoring systems. These are all subjects the trapper should understand and be well versed in before venturing into the field to trap bobcats.

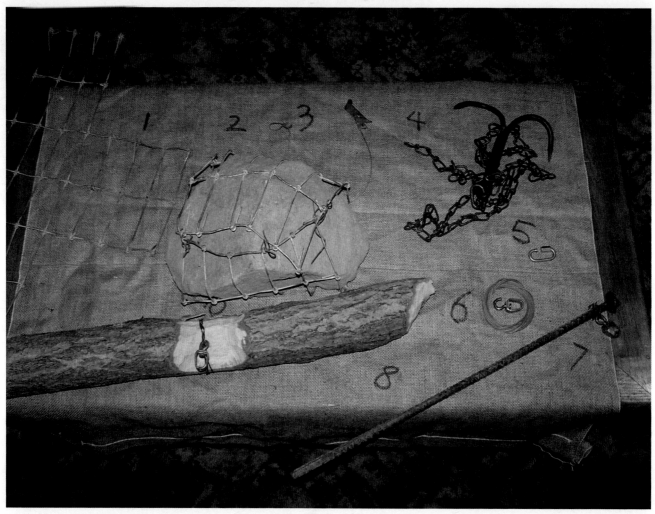

My anchoring systems: 1-Net fencing cut into a t shape to wrap and hold rock drags.
2- Rock drag ready to go, 3- Berkshire cable stake 4-Grapple drag and chain. 5- Quick-link for hooking up anchoring systems. 6- Cable slide system shown on page 44. 7-rebar stake 8-Log drag made from a natural beaver cut log

I will discuss the anchoring systems first because this will determine the depth of your trap bedding hole. If you will be using a grapple type drag you will need room below the trap to place the grapple, cover it with some dirt then coil the chain attached to the drag, add some more dirt to bed the trap properly. In some situations I will not bury the grapple drag under the trap but dig a small trench and bed the grapple and chain behind the backing or under some brush used to block and narrow the set down to one narrow trail.

If using a rebar stake or cable stake, you only need to dig out a trap bed that is just big enough to allow the trap to sit ¼ to ½ inch below the ground level. When you are just starting out, you may have to set the trap in the hole and make sure it will fit right. After you have the bed just big enough to hold the trap, the next step is to hammer the stake into the ground right in the center of the hole you have made to set the trap. If you are using a rebar stake, place the stake through the trap ring and hammer it into the ground. If you are using a earth anchor, cable stake you can use a half hitch to attach the cable stake to the trap chain loop or attach the trap to the cable with a threaded,quick-link, once the stake is in the ground. If you are concerned about possible trap theft, use the half hitch. A thief will need a cable stake puller, cable cutter or shovel to steal your trap.

If I am going to use a log drag, rock drag or grapple type drag, I will use 6 to 8 foot of chain attached to the trap chain. Rather than have this chain already attached to my traps, I prefer to have some loose chain cut to lengths and some lengths of chain attached to grapple drags then use quick links or wire to attach these drags to my traps in the field. In this way, I don't have a set number of traps already committed to a particular set up. I can have all my traps the same

and chose the anchoring system as I need it in the field. This keeps things much more organized. Traps with a bunch of chain already attached, has a tendency to get tangled up and disorganized.

Once the anchoring system is chosen, the trap bed made, the next thing is to dig your dirt hole or arrange things so that the trap will be in the right location for a bobcat to step on the pan. With a dirt hole or flat set I like my trap pan to sit 6 inches from the edge of the hole or cow skull or backing edge if I am using a rock or even just a tuft of grass. Make sure the trap dog is toward the dirt hole

My friend Neil Griffin remaking a bobcat flat set.

or backing.Once you are ready to cover the trap, bed your grapple and chain making sure the grapple is not tangled in the chain, add an inch of dirt over the chain and bed the trap solidly so that there is no movement in the trap. You can test this by pushing down on the edges of the trap. It should not move **at all**. If it moves a little, pack more dirt around the trap and wiggle in until it sets firmly. You can step on the trap edges, with your boots and wiggle it in tight if you are careful to avoid the trap pan.   Bedding your trap solidly is the single most important habit a trapper can make to ensure a solid paw catch. Trappers that do not learn to do this will constantly educate animals, lose animals or or make poor paw catches. Poor catches result in injured animals or lost animals. If a predator working the set steps on the edge of the trap and it wiggles under his foot, you will alarm the critter and most likely not catch it. If the trap

wiggles just before going off, the bobcat will jerk its foot back and the trap will either miss or just catch a toe or two.

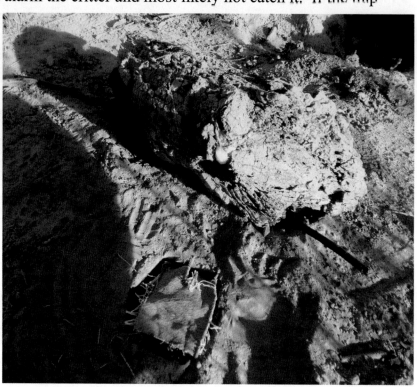

Once the trap is bedded solidly, you can place a pan cover over the pan to keep dirt out from under the trap pan. You can use a pan capper and bed the trap right up to the pan, or you can use a foam trap pan protector or some insulation under the pan to keep dirt and small rocks from getting under your trap pan. I have been trapping for over 30 years and I have tried everything. The thing that works best for me may not work best for you. Soil types determine the system that will work best for you. The soil in the areas I trap is very sandy. If I do

The pan cover of choice for me, old levi's cut to form

not use a trap pan cover, sand will slowly settle in around and under the trap pan and can prevent the trap from going off. I use pan covers cut from old pairs of levi pants to cover my trap pans in dry weather, and wax paper that I cut to size, for periods of wet weather. Wax paper will not soak up water and freeze. It is helpful to wad up the wax paper pan cover and then flatten it again before using it, to take some of the crisp, sound out of the paper.

In areas with nice loamy soil a trap capper can be used to pack dirt all around the trap and right up the the pan. I choose to not use anything under the pan of my traps because moisture can seep into a foam protector or some building insulation then freeze like a rock under your pan, and prevent a trap from going off. Building insulation has a peculiar smell to it and I know if I can smell it, the animals can. In areas that I trap, where pack rats are present, they dig around the trap pan and steal the insulation, when I have used it in the past. I know they can smell it because they keep stealing it until I use a different trap covering! Using this to protect your trap pans on bobcat sets is probably a pretty safe bet in dry areas of the country, but because of my experiences I try to use the system that has caused the least overall problems and make it universal on my trap line.

After your pan cover is in place, and you have carefully noted the position of your trap pan, use a trap sifter and sift over your set covering it with around ¼ inch of dirt. It is helpful to have a two inch wide soft bristled paint brush to smooth things around and keep everything flat. Use dirt clods, small rocks or sticks to use as stepping guides around your set to show the bobcat where to put his foot, even though if you have everything set up right, the trap pan should already be the natural spot a bobcat would step to investigate your set.

Make sure to keep all rocks and sticks away from the trap jaws or they could prevent the trap from closing on the animals foot, or give it enough room to slide free. Sooner or later it will happen to every trapper and they will find a small stick or rock wedged in the trap jaws and a few hairs telling of a near miss because of a misplaced stepping guide or the animal bumping the stepping guide into the pattern. For this reason I commonly use small dirt clods as my stepping guides. They

Sifting dirt over a walk-through bobcat set.

will cause the animal to step where I want it to step, but will disintegrate in a closing trap.

Once your trap is set and covered add bait to the dirt hole a small glob of scent to the lip of the hole and a shot of bobcat urine to the backing. On most dirt hole sets I will use bobcat gland lure as my scent. Sometimes I will use a curiosity lure such as beaver castor or cat nip. In very cold weather I am inclined to use some scent with a light musky or skunky smell. I don't often use a long distance call type lure directly in a dirt hole set for two reasons. It is usually to over powering for the animal to work the set properly, and if the animal gets this scent on its fur when it gets caught, it is not good! I save my very strong and skunky lures for use in a tall backing, tree or rock next to the set to bring the animal in where it will find the trap pattern. If it is very cold and snowy, using a LDC, (long distance call lure) right in a dirt hole or at your set may just the ticket to an animal finding your set and getting caught.

Now that your primary set is made, pick a location using the opposite wind direction principle and make a set 10 or 15 feet away. It is a good practice to make this set with fox and coyote in mind. Make a smaller dirt hole and use a different scent in the hole and some red fox urine over and behind the dirt hole. Another great option is to just make a urine post set using a fist sized rock or natural bush, stick or grass clump. If your predominate canine predator is the coyote set your trap a foot in front of the post and give a shot of coyote urine or fox urine up against the post from the trap side. Set the trap facing the most likely direction of approach, for instance a trail or the direction toward the primary bobcat set. A dog coyote that identifies a urine post will sniff at it then run up along side of it and urinate on it. A female will sniff it then turn and squat near it. With your trap set 12 inches directly in front of the spot the urine was applied, you can catch the coyote as it comes up to smell it or when it runs up or turns to urinate.

If you do not have many coyotes in your area and red fox is the predominate predator then set your trap so the pan is 6 inches in front of the post to target the smaller fox.

I touched on the subject earlier in this book but it is worth mentioning again here. Try to envision what a bobcat is doing when he visits the location you have chosen to make your sets, and then make sets that will naturally appeal to his actions.

Two things to think about with every set are 1- Will the bobcat see my set as he is traveling? Is it right on his travel route? 2- Will the bobcat smell my set? Is it on the up wind side of the trail or travel path?

Red fox caught at a back up set near a bobcat set.

At most bobcat set locations I will back up the first trap with a second, back-up set. I do this for three reasons. First you sometimes catch a rabbit or some other non target animal. If a bobcat comes along, he will get a free meal without getting caught himself. If you have a back up set you will often catch a bobcat as he looks things over, or explores around after eating his meal. Reason number two is that sometimes you will catch two bobcats, particularly during the breeding season when bobcats are traveling in pairs. You may want to turn the female loose, but if she gets caught first you will never have a chance at the tom if you don't have a second set. You could also catch a double of a fox and bobcat or bobcat and coyote, or some other predator combination. All of this is putting more fur on the stretcher and money in your pocket. The third reason to make a back up set is because the sets you will be making for bobcats do not target red fox or coyote. They will locate your bobcat sets but because of the nature of the set, may not work the pattern. A back up set from 10 to 20 feet away, made specifically to target fox and coyote is a deadly thing. Coyotes and foxes will locate the bobcat

34

set, be suspicious, circle around and locate the more subtle set that is a small ,blended in dirt hole or urine post set. This set is much less intimidating to them and there is a high likelihood that they will get caught here.

There is another reason for a back-up set that not too many folks consider. You should always try to make all your sets so that the predominate wind direction will take the scent to the traveling animal, but what happens when the wind is blowing from a different direction, as often happens in the winter with approaching storms and unpredictable weather? A back up set can and should be made with the opposite wind direction in mind. Think about it, if the predominate

A big tom caught on a trail set.

wind direction is from the west and you have made your set along a trail running north and south and made your dirt hole on the west side of the trail, any traveling cat will smell the set if the wind is blowing from its predominate direction. If the wind would happen to blow from the north or south, the set is close enough to the trail that some of the scent will reach the animal if it is traveling north or south, but if the wind is blowing from the east the cat may never scent the set. A back up set on the east side of the trail and 10 feet away from the first set will pick up the animal, or cause it to circle and locate the predominate set and get caught. At any rate the back-up increases your odds in so many ways that I seldom make a single set at any good bobcat location. By changing the back-up set to a more subtle set focusing on the canines, you will increase your catch or pick up a bobcat that didn't locate the primary set because of wind direction or a miscalculation of where a cat should travel.

Dirt Hole Set

This type of set is used more in predator trapping than any other. For most dirt hole sets I will use a rebar stake or cable stake anchoring system. Dirt hole sets can be easily remade and the scent from a trapped animal and the scratched up ground is great eye appeal. The only reason I would use a different trap anchoring system would be if the animal might be visible to hikers or other passer-byes. Remember if people may be in the area they may have a dog with them and this opens a can of worms I prefer to avoid.

For targeting bobcats the dirt hole should be different than the set you would use to target coyote or fox. The best coyote or fox dirt hole is a dirt hole with slight step down with the right distance for the target animal, from the trap to the hole. For a coyote this is around ten inches. For targeting farmland fox I use a step down four or five inches in front of the hole. I don't recommend a step down for bobcat but rather a flat approach and bigger dirt hole pattern. I use stepping guides to put the bobcat's foot 5-6 inches in front of the dirt hole. It is nice to use a little backing such as a tuft of grass, cow pie, bush or rock to use in making the set but it is not

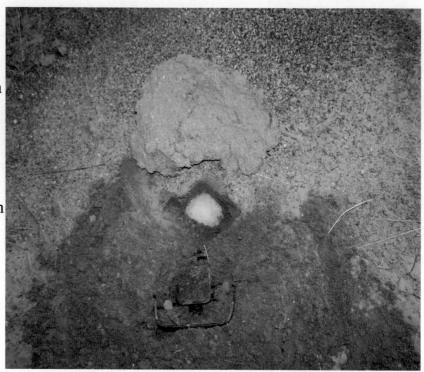

Unfinished dirt hole set with cotton used in the hole

necessary. It you have the angle of your hole at 45-60% the bobcat cannot see into the hole without moving to the front and stepping on the trap pan. I like to use a little cotton or white

batting in the hole on top of the bait or scent to look like some white fur. This contrast will give the cat some eye appeal and add to his curiosity.

Another thing I do differently from a coyote set is really throw the dirt around make scratch marks and do not blend the fresh dirt into the surrounding dirt. I want things to stand out and look disturbed. I use small rocks from the trap bed or little sticks or pine cones as stepping guides to force the bobcat to step directly on the trap pan as it investigates the hole. I usually put a chunk of bait into the bottom of a 6-10 inch deep hole,

Finished dirt hole set from above.

that is two or three inches in diameter. Set along a game trail

Put a plug of cotton or pillow stuffing in on top the bait then some gland lure and urine to the backing or top edge of the hole. This makes the dirt hole look like another animal's food stash and brings out the competitive drive as well as food attraction. If this set is made right along the travel path of a bobcat and on the upwind side of the trail, any passing bobcat or other predator will see the hole, smell the lure and bait and investigate.

The Flat Set

Nice bobcat caught at the dirt hole set above.

Another great set for bobcats along a trail or hunting travel area is a flat set with some sort of interesting attraction. I like some bigger bleached cow bones or an old deer or cow skull, something that really stands out and will get a bobcat's attention. A piece of firewood placed along the trail where nothing has been before will also have the desired effect. With this type of set I like to place scent in the eye hole or the cow skull with the scented hole facing the trap, which is 6 inches from the skull. I use some stepping guides to put the cat's foot firmly on the trap pan. sprinkle urine on top the skull and call it good. Once again I put in a

Nice tom caught at a flat set that was a a pack rat nest!

back up set with the wind direction and canines in mind. I make subtle dirt hole, and only use urine or gland lure. I may even just use a coyote dropping and some urine and blend the trap in.

Occasionally I will use a flag at a bobcat set location. I like to use fake fur of different colors to contrast with the brush and existing conditions. White is my favorite color if there is no snow on the ground. In snow conditions I use dark brown or black flags. I want colors that contrast to the back ground. I also want my flags to move easily and flutter in the wind. To accomplish this I like to hinge my flags with two loops of wire.

Some great locations for a flag set is up against a brush line where a trail is passing along the front. Here you have a convenient place to cut out a little semi-protected shelter and have overhanging sticks to hang your flag from. I prefer to have my flags toward the back of my set so that a cat has to pass over the trap to get to the flag. I have experimented with flag height and I feel that 4 feet is about the right height to hang a bobcat flag. I want the bobcat to feel he can actually get to the flag

Badger caught at a flagged bobcat set: Notice black flag.

without jumping. This seems to encourage them to check it out. Sets like this can be made to keep out snow and moisture by placing pine bows or other brush above the set.

Another great location for a flag set is at the junction of several trails in a saddle. You do not need to set every trail, just find a location where the trails all come together and the wind direction is right and put up a tripod of sticks that reaches 6-8 feet in the air, like a small tee pee. Hang the flag from the center so it hangs down about 4 feet from the ground and is visible in every direction, and set a trap directly under the flag. Use some stepping guides to show the cat where to place his feet and use some gland lure to the left on the ground, urine to the right, and some LDC, **long distance call** lure up on the top of the tripod. Don't forget your back up set with the opposite wind direction and coyotes in mind.

Large trees with low hanging canopies are another great location for a flagged bobcat set. With this type of set I will lay two wrist sized branches against the tree from about three feet up on the trunk and angled down to the ground, forming a V-shaped cubby. I add some smaller branches and sticks to block off every approach but from the front. Hang my flag in the back of the set up 4 feet or so and set the bobcat trap so that the cat has to pass across the trap to get to the scent and flagging at the rear of the set. I like to narrow the bobcats approach inside the cubby, and use dirt clods, pine cones or small sticks to put the cat's foot right on the trap pan.

I use a lot of flagged bobcat sets when I am trapping cats in ledge country. In this situation a flag can serve a two fold purpose. It can act as a main attraction to a cat traveling along the ledge, but it can also be incorporated into the set in such a way that when a catch is made the flag is pulled down and serves as an indicator that a catch has been made. You can accomplish this by wrapping length of chain around a stick that is holding up the flag, or you can actually wire the flag to the trap chain so it will be pulled down when a bobcat or other animal struggles in the trap. This type of set up can save you so much leg work

Spotted skunk caught at a flagged bobcat set. Notice the stick by the skunk that was leaned up, wrapped with chain, and used to indicate a catch when it was tipped over.

and time that is goes without saying. I also use a back up set in the ledges for reasons I mentioned earlier. You will not catch many coyotes or red fox here, but plenty of gray fox, ringtail cats, spotted skunks will get into trap sets made in rocky or ledgy country, so make back up sets here too.

The Toilet Set

A bobcat toilet set is as close to a guaranteed catch as can be made with a bobcat. Visible evidence that a bobcat is using an area as a toilet, almost guarantees that it will be back on a regular basis. When your setting traps at a bobcat toilet, you should not disturb anything. Treat the area with great care and just blend in a trap and add some bobcat urine and gland lure to a bobcat dropping picked up in another area. Here you are appealing to the territorial and sexual instinct of a bobcat, and you can actually ruin a good toilet by trying to make a dirt hole set or flag set at this location. Bobcats do not just randomly pick toilet locations. These are key territorial features. They do not like them messed with or reconstructed. I discovered this the hard way on many occasions as a young trapper. It finally dawned on me after one big tom I was after would not go back to a toilet location where I tried to create a walk-through set out of his toilet. He simply made a new toilet a few hundred feet away and avoided my walk-through. I slipped in a trap at his new toilet, added a fresh bobcat turd from another area on my trap line. Gave it a shot of gland lure and bobcat urine and had the big tom on my next trap check! Over the next few years other tom cats took over the toilet and by careful preservation of the location I still regularly catch nice tom cats here.

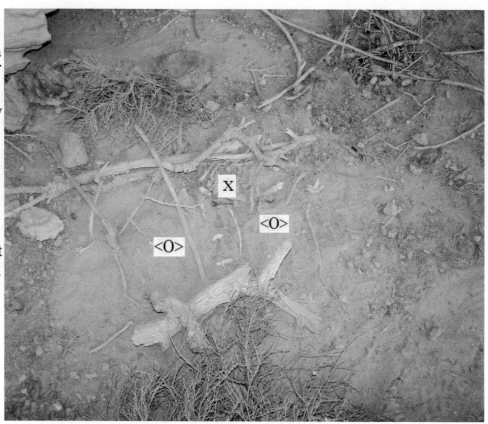

Nice toilet set with traps at <O> and gland lure at X

The Walk-Through Set

Use a walk-through sets for areas you see a bobcat's tracks coming and going. Narrow places in a trail, or where a cat is walking up under a ledge. Places they are naturally traveling areas where things are narrowed up are great lotions. Here is is fine to narrow things up even more and use stepping guides to make the cat step on the trap pan. On most walk-trough sets I do not use any scent of bait. I want the cat to be naturally walking through the set, going forward.

Nice walk-through bobcat set with an antler as attraction.

40

You can get creative if you have a good location for a walk-through, such as a dry ledge near a game trail. You can try to pull a bobcat off the trail with a flag then get him to walk through the set toward some scent or bait. What you don't want is to use scent or bait in the walk-through. What will happen is you will cause the bobcat to stop and carefully place his feet in unnatural positions as he attempts to investigate things. His natural momentum and your carefully placed stepping guides may well become platforms for him to put his feet on. If you attempt this you will toe catch some cats, catch them by their hind feet or miss them all-together and now you have a spooked, educated bobcat that will avoid this set type and the scent or bait you used. It is effective to create a walk through set into a cave or narrow area by placing bait or scent on the interior, but don't attempt to stop a bobcats forward movement at a walk-through set. You want a natural lane with the bobcat putting even weight on its feet as it travels through and on top of the trap pan.

Walk-through set with traps at <O> and Long distance call lure at X

Log Crossing Set

Along most trap lines you will have special features where you can catch a bobcat. One of these locations is where a log lays across a stream or creek that is difficult for a bobcat to cross without getting wet. You can even cut and place a log in a location like this prior to the season while you are scouting so the animals can find and use it. Remember to make notches in the log where you will set your traps and fill the notches with dirt where you will later put your trap and blend it in. You can make this crossing even better by lashing two smaller logs together and putting dirt and leaves to smooth out the surface and make a place for traps. This also makes it possible for you to cross the river without waders if you choose.

Set traps on both ends of the crossing about 4 feet in and you can make multiple catches! I like to use a one-way beaver cable slide to either drown animals in deep water or slide them away from the crossing and up into the brush along the bank. This will encourage multiple catches and keep animals from messing up the crossing.

41

Cubby sets are used predominately in the north country to catch lynx. They work just as effectively for bobcats. The great thing about cubby's is they can be constructed to be weather proof. You can use a black plastic garbage bag or any type of plastic sheeting incorporated into the construction to make a weather proof roof. In some areas this is the only set that will keep working in deep snow-covered landscapes. Another great thing about a cubby is it will work very well for a foot-hold trap or a snare or conibear type, kill trap. Plastic 5 gallon buckets can be effective cubby's for bobcats when screwed to a tree a foot off the ground. With bait in the back

Natural type cubby set up with a body grip trap and bait.

and a conibear trap in the front, you will nab most passing bobcats, not to mention some coyotes, fox, fisher or whatever other predators frequent your woods!

Cave sets are best treated like walk-through sets and can employ a trap, snare or conibear, body grip, trap near the entrance where you use brush, sticks and rocks to narrow up the entrance. A bit of bait in the back of the cave and some long distance call lure on the outside top edge of the cave will encourage exploration.

Snares are effective tools for bobcats in many of the same sets I have mentioned before. They are especially effective when incorporated into walk-through sets, trail sets, or semi-cubby, flag sets, under brush or trees.

When you have settled on some good areas to trap the next thing you should start doing is picking out trap locations and determining what type of anchoring system you will use for each trap location. Because some set locations, like a dirt hole or flat set can easily be rebuilt and the destruction of the set actually serves as a great curiosity to the next bobcat, you can use a cable stake or rebar stake or some other way of anchoring the trap right at the set locations. In some situations such as a toilet set or a walk-through set that you do not want destroyed or messed up the best thing is to employ a grapple drag, log or rock drag.

I will discuss each of these sets and the systems in detail in a future chapter but a little insight here is good. The basic dirt hole set is employed at about 25% of my bobcat sets. I make this set along bobcat travel routes in areas that bobcats hunt. Some ideal locations are two track road edges and just off trails on the upwind side and occasionally in a saddle crossing as a secondary set. At most dirt holes I will use a rebar stake or cable stake to anchor the trap or traps. If the road or trail is actively used by outdoorsmen or hikers, I will use a drag or cable slide system, to allow bobcats to move away from the travel location and off into the brush and out of sight.

About 50% of my sets are walk-through sets. This set is made to narrow up a place bobcats are actively traveling and put their foot right on the trap pan with the use of stepping guides such as rocks and sticks. Because this is a constructed set that I do not want destroyed I use a log drag, rock drag or grapple type drag to attach the trap. When a bobcat is caught it will mess up the location a little bit but if the drag is at the edge of

A nice weather proof cave set that has produced a lot of bobcats over the years.

43

the set, the bobcat will usually move away from the set and tangle in the brush, without to much damage to the location.

The remaining 25% of my sets are a variety of specialty sets adapted to the areas I trap. I use flat sets with a curiosity attraction like an old cow skull. I use a flagged set at a wider saddle when I am not exactly sure where a bobcat will travel through. Cave sets are created in areas where caves and overhanging rocks exist. Stream crossing sets are made where a log or beaver dam allows a bobcat or other predator to cross a stream without getting wet. Scratch post and scent post sets are made when a tree or log is found that bobcats use to sharpen their claws and mark their territory. A cubby set is used by making a small man made cave, and works great in snow country, to keep your sets dry and functioning.

At flat sets and scratch posts I like to keep my cats right where they are trapped. They tear things up, leave a lot of scent and eye appeal and the sets are easily remade by smoothing things up, digging out the hole and re bedding the trap. For this reason I use a cable stake at a flat set and a 1 ¾ fencing staple to anchor my trap directly to the scratch post tree.

At a cave set and cubby set I like to use a heavy log drag or grapple drag to keep the cat from destroying my cubby or jumping out of the cave at me when I check the trap! At a flagged set I use which ever anchoring system works best for the set up. If I have my flag hanging from a limb of a tree, I often anchor the trap directly to the tree with a fencing staple, If I use a triangle of sticks to hold up my flag, such as in a saddle where several trails intersect, I will use a rock, log or grapple drag if there is enough brush and rocks to tangle things up and prevent a bobcat from leaving the immediate area, while preserving my set for the remake.

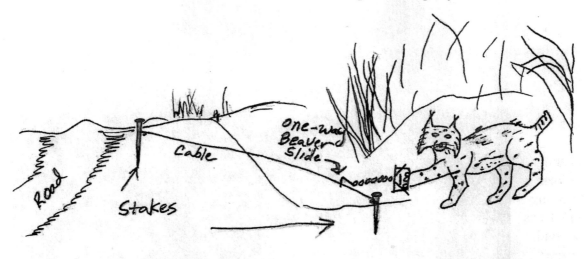

Use this keen set-up to slide a trapped bobcat off a road or trail and into the brush so it will not be seen. Trapped bobcats hide very well if given a chance to have some cover.

There are a lot of great trapping spots that visibility of a trapped animal is an issue. I have used this set up many times to prevent potential problems.

At any rate what I am trying to get you thinking about is while your in the field you can carry some anchoring systems with you in your back pack and when you find a likely place to set a trap you can pound a stake, locate a log or rock for a drag, set up your walk-through sets, minus the trap, drop the log across the stream for a log crossing set, locate the caves, over hangs and bobcat toilets and pretty much get everything ready to just add your trap, scent and bait, hang your flags and add a little eye appeal in the way of feathers and scratch marks. If your time in the field during trapping season is dedicated to actually just putting traps in the ground and checking traps you will save time and it help you catch more animals in a shorter time.

A big part of field work is being prepared for inclement weather conditions or with a back up plan if weather gets really seviere. To remake trap sets after rain or snow you will need access to dry dirt. I fill several 50 gallon drums with dry dirt during the summer months and store it in a shed for trapping use in bad weather. I also have areas like old barns and big dry caves where I can obtain more dry dirt if it is needed.

Big cedar trees make nice dry trap sets for winter weather.

Another part of field work is doing your homework and knowing if bobcats migrate or move to different areas during the trapping season months of winter. In most areas I trap, bobcats move very little between summer and winter seasons.   I trap the western desert country and lower mountain foothills. Some years these areas get quite a lot of snow but the broken country offers plenty of options for keeping my traps working. There are plenty of overhanging cliffs, caves, large over hanging trees, and natural cubbys. In bad snow years I will employ many man made cubbys made of sticks, flat rocks or old 50 gallon drums.

During periods of prolonged bad weather or snowy conditions, bobcats will spend more time, or altogether move to, south facing slopes and near rocks for protection from wind and moisture.

In mountainous regions all game may migrate to lower wintering areas or move to more remote south facing slopes. If you didn't do your homework, your traps may sit under a couple of feet of snow and miles away from the bobcats and other furbearcrs in lower country.

In low-land timbered country such as the Eastern US. Heavy snow can cover the landscape but animals stay right where they are and make do. In these areas constructed cubby's of logs, rock or plywood, 50 gallon drums, or even baited, five gallon buckets with a snare or conibear trap can stay operational and be very effective, while these conditions last.

Anything that can be done in the field or at home prior to trapping season starting should be done. As soon as the season opens you should be focusing on getting your traps put into your set locations and checking traps. Then your evenings will be busy skinning, fleshing and stretching your furs!

You will find you can increase your odds from the very first day of the season by moving in quietly, setting your traps and moving out. If you have to pound stakes, make a big disturbance and leave a lot of human scent, it will scare animals out of the area and take bobcats longer to get into your sets.

Remember south slopes are always better for winter trapping, even if there is no snow. All creatures like to be in the sun on cold winter days. Predators and prey animals will seek sunny spots to relax. Deer and rodents will find some green shoots and better feed in sunny spots. For most of the summer animals hold to the cooler north slopes where the snow has set longer and grasses receive

Fox caught in small cave and pulled log drag out away from set more moisture and grow taller all summer. Usually by late fall or early winter these areas have been grazed off. It just stands to reason that now the sunny south slopes would be the places animals would look for food.

Be prepared for snow and rain conditions with plenty of stored or available dry dirt for making your sets. A cheap and effective anti-freeze is plain old table salt. I use the one pound cardboard cans with a pour spout and sprinkle salt on the set while I am making it and after it is done. If you can get by with dry dirt and weather-proof sets you you will be better off, but if things are just cold and not too wet, using table salt will keep your sets working.

It is wise to have half of your sets weather proof for bobcats, if your area gets a lot of snow. You can use man made cubbys, natural caves and bushy trees, the underside of dry bridges and culverts, 50 gallon drums, caves dug back in a bank, or old abandoned cabins to make dry sets. Bait is particularly appealing in these types of sets, because cold weather will keep it fresh and appealing to bobcats.

Make your cubbys and set your buckets or 55 gallon drums out before the season and make sure they have enough dry dirt in the bottom to cover traps. Trying to carry drums or gear on icy, snow-covered slopes, is just asking for a fall, so this is another good reason to prepare prior to the season.

Trap Selection and Maintenance

With any type of business you are limited by the quality and effectiveness of your equipment and tools. A trapper is only as good as his traps and equipment allow him to be. If you are starting out I would recommend that you purchase and use only #3 double coil-spring traps for trapping bobcats. My second choice would be #2 double coil-spring traps, but I would only use these traps in sandy soil and in areas that do not get significant rain or snow fall. (Or if required by law to obtain a specific trap dimension).

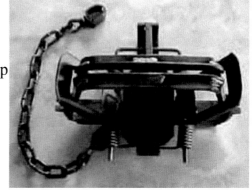

I would also recommend that all your traps be 4 coiled and the jaws have an off-set gap and outside jaw lamination. You can see the photo of the #3 double coil spring, four coiled off-set trap in the photo. This is the trap I now use exclusively for bobcats and coyotes on my trap line. This trap is lightening fast, can break through wet and semi frozen soil, gets a good firm foot catch and does not damage an animals foot. The extra money spent on these traps will more than pay for themselves the first season they are used. Carefully cleaned and stored out of the weather, these traps will last for a lifetime. You may need to periodically replace a pan, dog or springs but this is a minimal cost.

Bridger # 3 modified
My favorite bobcat trap

Before I clean and wax new traps I like to make sure they are properly tuned. To properly tune traps you will need a metal file with a square edge. A pair of pliers and a phillips screwdriver. I first examine the dog notch to make sure it is flat and not rounded. I like to file the face of the dog holder notch down just a little and make it good and square. I then set the pan tension to about 2 lbs using the phillips screwdriver and pliers to tighten the pan nut. There is a tool you can buy to check the exact poundage. I have done it for so many years I know just how much tension to apply. After I have the pan set with the resistance I want, I set the trap and make sure the pan sets flat. Using a handy 2 foot stick or 1"x1" x 2' foot wood scrap set the trap off slowly watching for any creep of the pan downward as you put pressure on it. If you see any creep in the pan at all, the dog notch is too deep or the dog itself is too long. One year I bought some #4 Duke traps and I had to crimp the dog loop a little then file every dog down by nearly 1/8" before they were the right length to allow the trap to snap shut without the pan creeping downward first. If the pan is too low or humped up, you may have to move the dog swivel holder in or out with your pliers. Try to adjust everything first to get the trap flat and firing all at once before filing or modifying things.

I don't use long spring traps for predator trapping anymore. They are very hard on an animals foot because they are so bulky and do not easily swivel. They are very slow compared to a 4 coiled trap. They are also difficult to bed and do not come standard with a pan tension adjustment. These traps work great for beaver traps, or any drowning set for raccoon or otter.

The conibear traps that I use I treat just like my #3 coil spring traps. I clean them, and boil them in my trap tea, but I do not wax them. They are dangerous enough as they are without making them super slick, especially around the trigger mechanism.

New snares should be boiled in a mild solution of baking soda to take any oil or shipping contaminates off and give them a dull look. You should put a little memory in each snare before you use them. I like to open and close them a few times bend a little here and there to get a nice round shape when they are opened. Next, I like to wax my snares because it makes them work more smoothly and takes away the steel odor. Of course most snares that catch a bobcat or coyote are pretty well thrashed. Some of them can be reused and of course recycle the locks, and break-away clips for building new snares.

I do not dye my traps with a commercial trap dye like many trappers recommend. I merely boil new traps to remove the shipping oil, then boil them again in leaves, bark and vegetation that is found on my trapline. I personally use sagebrush leaves and bark, cedar needles and berries and some oak bark. After boiling my new traps in this natural tea of vegetation, they take on a gray hue. When they are dry I heat up some trap

From Left: An old turkey fryer I use to wax traps Two 55 gallon drums, one with a drain installed. This is the set up I use to boil and wax traps

48

wax and wax the new traps. Every year prior to trapping season I clean up my traps with a power washer. Boil them to remove the remaining wax, then boil them again in my natural tea. Within a few years my traps are as dark as any commercial dyed traps, and they do not rust.

The key to keep your traps in mint condition is to store them away from moisture and remove any rust that has developed during the season, prior to storing them. I like to clean, boil and then wax all my traps right after the season ends. This is a fun spring project and my traps are all ready to go for the next trapping season.

This is a propane burner I use to boil and wax traps.

During the season, some traps get exposed to anti-freeze, moisture and get beat up catching bobcats and coyotes. If you have a bunch of traps that need to be cleaned and touched up, wash them with a power washer or take them to a car wash and wash them with hot water, let them dry then heat some wax, dip the traps until they are hot then hang them up and let the wax harden. This quick clean and wax session will get rid of odors and help prevent your traps from starting to rust during the wettest most abusive trapping season.

Trap Anchoring Systems

On my trap line I use five types of anchoring devices. For staking traps solid I use cable stakes. These stakes are a more recent invention that allows a sharpened length of steel with a length of looped cable attached to the center of the device. When this is driven down into the ground and **set,** by pulling up sharply on the cable end, the device turns lengthwise in the ground as the pressure on the anchor point forces the device to attempt to come out of the ground lengthwise. Cable stakes are lighter to carry than rebar stakes, and have far greater holding power. It takes a special stake puller to get these out of the ground. I have invented my own cable stake system made from short lengths of cut rebar. They will drive into rocky or hard ground. The only draw back with my design is that sometimes fine sand will jam the stake into the driver. This happens so seldom I scarcely have to worry about it. Usually with a quick twist of the driver handles the stake releases and I can set it with a quick jerk. These are the absolutely toughest, sharpest and least expensive cable stakes make and I use thousands of them on my trapline. In very fine or loose sand I prefer to use the Berkshire cable stakes with their wide body which creates more resistance in fine loose sand. With any cable stake system, the longer the cable and the further your drive it into the ground, the more resistance it will hold. I have tipped my four wheeler over trying to pull cable stakes out of the ground! I often have to leave my cable stakes that are driven into rocky ground because you cannot pull them out when they are wedged between two rocks.

Often I will make my bobcat sets around or under pinyon/juniper or various other types of trees. In this situation the simplest anchoring system is a 1 ¾ or 2" fencing staple. Make sure when anchoring traps to trees to: A-put the staple in solid wood. Rotten wood or some light woods like aspen won't hold well and you should wrap the chain around the tree in a half knot before nailing it to the tree. That way the chain is tightening on the tree like a dally and the staple doesn't need to hold a lot of pressure. B- Leave just enough distance between the staple

and trap chain to get your fence pliers, staple puller end started so you can remove your trap when your done. This allows the staple to be pulled.

A unique anchoring system that can be cleverly employed is borrowed from the beaver trapline. It is called a one-way cable slide. In beaver trapping this system is usually between a heavy rock thrown into deep water a length or cable and a stake pounded into the bank near your trap. A one way beaver slide

My cable anchoring system made with rebar and a ½" steel nipple.

Well hidden trapped bobcat!

is attached to the trap, or the trap chain end swivel with a hole in the end, will also work great if the cable from the direction of where you want the trapped bobcat to end up, is slid through the hole from the inside, (near the swivel end). The beaver will fight the trap and then dive for deep water and will be unable to surface and drown.

When used for bobcat trapping, this system can be used to slide a bobcat off a road edge or trail and into the brush out of sight. It could be used at a log crossing set to make a drowning set or to slide the bobcat off the log and into the brush line so that another catch can be made on a second trap set on the other end of the log crossing. If could also be used anywhere you have a set location that you do not want destroyed such as a toilet set, and there is not enough brush or obstacles to tangle a bobcat with a drag or grapple.

The last type of anchoring system I use is the drag anchoring system. This anchor is used to allow a trapped bobcat to move away from the set location and get tangled up in the brush out of sight. I only employ this type of anchor when there is sufficient brush, trees or rocks to ensure the bobcat does not go very far before getting tangled up. For this type of set up you need 6 to 8' of welded link chain and the drag. I use three types of drags, logs, rocks and a welded steel grapple. For anchoring to a log I use some bailing wire and a fencing staple. For anchoring to a 15 or 20lb rock, I use a wire cross made from net fencing. I wrap the wire around and tied it off with bailing wire, then I use a quick link to

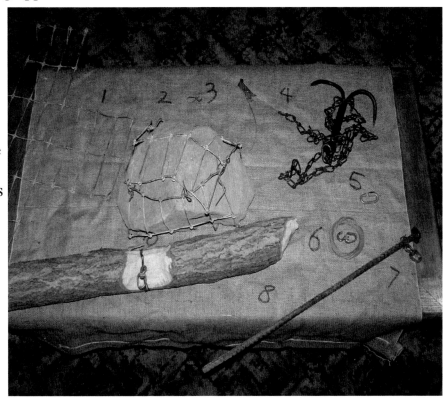

Another look at my anchoring systems, 1) My net wraps for rock drags, 2) Net wrap in place, 3)Berkshire cable stake, 4) Grapple drag and 8' chain, 5) Quick-link for hooking up anchors 6) Cable slide system shown on page 44. 7) rebar stake 8) Log drag made from a beaver cut log.

anchor this to the 8' of trap chain. With this system the rock cannot come loose like it can when you just try to wire your trap chain directly to a rock. The wire digs into the ground and leaves a good drag mark to follow.

Grapple drags are nice to use and work very well but are expensive to buy and time consuming to make. They can be buried right at your sets and really have a great advantage on a coyote trap line where you want all your trap and hardware out of sight to the cunning coyote. With a bobcat this is not necessary, and I often just poke my grapple drags up under some brush or leaves at the trap and don't worry about covering it with dirt.

The beauty for a drag system is that trapped animals can get away from the set location, get into cover and then get tangled out of sight of other animals and people. The only possible draw back is occasionally an animal will travel quite a distance before getting tangled up or become caught before a snow storm or rain storm and the drag marks covered or wiped out. Because of this it is imperative that you make sure the chain is not hooked or tangled in the drag while making your set, and that you check your drag sets just before any seviere storm.

Other Types of Bobcat Traps

In some areas of the country, harsh winters are the norm. Snow covers the landscape and makes foot hold trapping difficult or impossible. In these areas, cubby sets and conibear traps are the ticket to trapping bobcats. Man made boxes, natural caves or constructed shelters made of sticks and tree boughs can be set up to hold the conibear trap at the entrance. With some bait and scent toward the back of the shelter and some powerful call scent above the set, these trap sets in a good bobcat travel area are very deadly. Your tracks in the snow going from set to set will make a natural travel route for bobcats to follow.

Deadly body grip set on a bobcat trail. Stock Photo

Bucket cubby: I like to screw these to a tree along a trail with fresh meat inside

There are considerations to be made with conibear traps since these traps will kill any animal that sticks its head into the set. Dogs and house cats will be killed just as easily as a bobcat or beaver by these powerful traps, and a human or child can be seriously injured. Follow your state laws and recommendations and follow all safety precautions while setting and handling these killer traps. Do not use them near parking or recreational areas and talk to private property owners before using them on their land. In the right area and situation a conibear trap is the very best weather proof, tool for trapping a bobcat.

Snares are also a great weather-proof tool for catching bobcats. In addition to the cubby sets mentioned   Bobcat snare set in a natural cubby above, snares can be set in trails that bobcats are using.
With a snare set, break away clips, designed
to open when a certain force is applied or stops should be used that prevents a snare from fully

closing, to ensure that deer and other big game animals do not get caught by their legs while walking on these trails. States that allow snares to be used will have specific instruction and regulations on how snares should be set up and used.

The use of a jump stick, (a stick placed to encourage deer and larger animals to jump over the snare, rather than brush through it is also helpful in many situations.

In three western states controlled by liberal politics, California, Arizona and Colorado, bobcat trappers must only use cage traps on state or public lands while trapping. I often trap in Arizona but avoid using cage traps in the areas I trap because I trap large private ranches or Indian reservations. I do use some cage traps and I encourage the bobcat trapper to have some cage traps for trapping bobcats and other critters near public areas and places that you may catch a domestic dog or house cat.

Cage traps are bulky to haul around, expensive and must be completely covered with brush and sticks and blended in to effectively catch bobcats and other animals.

The proper set up involves digging a hole in the ground just behind the spot the cage trap pan will set. This hole will hold your bait, bobcat gland lure and urine. Place the cage so the trap pan is directly in front of the hole you have dug. Cover the inside of the set trap with dirt up to the trap pan, to cover the wire floor. Carefully sprinkle some fine dirt on the trap pan. I like to actually glue a piece of roofing shingle on my cage trap pans or spray paint my pans with textured paint to hide the metal and give it a rough texture. I like to hang a piece of synthetic fur or a small white rag from a fishing line and swivel at the back of my traps. Beaver castor or catnip is a great natural scent to put on your flag.

After the trap is set, it is time to cover it with sticks brush and leaves and blend the set into the area so that it looks like a natural hole in the brush to a bobcat and escapes the notice of hikers or other people that may be using the area. You can add some long distance call lure in a tree or bush above your trap. If you have placed the trap right on a location that bobcats are using, this is not really necessary.

Notice I've covered the wire bottom with dirt. put some dirt on the pan and blended in the trap with vegetation. I have gland lure, urine and beaver castor in a dirt hole near the pan. I also have a cotton ball flag with a little skunk scent, hanging in the back.

Cage traps are very effective for catching bobcats when used in the fashion I have just described. In some areas you may be able to use feathers in your cage traps which really adds to their appeal for a bobcat. I like cage trapping, I just do not like the bulk of hauling traps around, the cost of each trap at $100 each and the inevitable theft when they are discovered by the public. In some areas of the country this is the only way you can trap. Good luck getting a coyote or red fox in a cage trap but bobcats, gray fox and other animals are easily caught so it is worth the effort once you overcome the initial investment to get the traps.

Nice Tom bobcat, Stock Photo

Trapping Tools

Just as with any other manual work or business, trapping requires a specific set of tools to make the job as smooth and quick as possible.

The first job in setting a trap is digging out the trap bed and anchoring your trap. The best tool for this job is a light single jack hammer/digging tool. This is a stake driving hammer with a piece of heavy flat plate welded to the back of the sledge and sharpened to an edge for easy digging and stake driving.

For digging out dirt holes there are many possible tools but I like a heavy duty steel trowel that is sturdy enough to use by hand or by driving it in with your hammer. One of the best I have is called a Jim Digger, by JC Conner. It has a 2 ¾ wide blade and is 23 inches long.

Every trapper needs to have is a cable stake driver. I have one that I make for my own system, that I use in rocky soils, and one that I use for the inexpensive Berkshire cable stakes I use in sandy soils.

There are many dirt sifting tools on the market, I like an all metal sifter with diamond cut screen. The one I use is 8"x10"x2 ¼" sold by Montgomery Fur Company. It is light weight but sturdy enough to scoop up dirt and will take most trapline abuse.

I keep a couple of pliers in my trapping tools. The standard side cutter/pliers combination is my go to pair, but I keep a pair of extension pliers for tightening pan bolts and fixing bent or stubborn parts. Sometimes a quick-link gets jammed up with dirt and won't open, and with the two pair of pliers you can make it cooperate!

A couple of sturdy screw drivers is also a trapline necessity. A regular screw driver is great for scraping dirt or mud from trap jaws or tightening old style pan tension screws. Most newer pan tension bolts take a phillips screw driver.

One tool that I use quite often, and can always be found in my trapping bag is a pair of fencing pliers. I use these to nail in and remove fence staples that I use to anchor traps to trees or fence posts.

For cutting limbs or clearing out brush I keep a small hand saw, which is on my leatherman that I always keep on my belt. You could choose to use a hatched for this work but I prefer the lighter saw.

To hold my tools I use a sturdy tool bag with a shoulder strap for hands-free carrying. In the winter when I haul dry dirt to my sets I also have a five gallon bucket for hauling dirt.

From left to right: Sifter, Jim Digger trowel, single jack with steel plate digger, Slip loc pliers, fencing pliers, side cutters, screw drivers cable stake driver and rebar stake. Other tools fencing staples, head lamp, trail camera, small LED spot light for checking traps.

Skinning and Fur Handling

Bobcat trapping is not over once you successfully snap the steel on a prime bobcat! In fact more money is lost at this phase of trapping than any other. Just as with any other furbearer, the bobcat must be dispatched, carefully and properly skinned, fleshed out and put on a fur form or stretcher. In some states you must remove the bottom jaw for analysis by a wildlife biologist from the state game department. Because these tasks are messy and time consuming, some trappers try to hurry or make easy work by cutting corners. Nothing will discourage you more than poor prices for improperly handled pelts, or a word of reprimand from an experienced fur handler. If you will carefully follow the guidelines I outline here, you will not experience these things. Always talk to your fur dealer and buyers at fur auctions to see how they want your furs put up, or to learn the latest techniques.

Once a bobcat is caught it must be properly dispatched. There really is only one good tool for doing this right and that is a dispatch stick, sometimes called a choke stick. I do carry a .22 pistol on my trap line for dispatching canines and critters that a dispatch stick won't work on, and to dispatch that occasional bobcat that is not caught very well and could escape while trying to get close enough to put the stick noose over the cat's head. If I choose to shoot a bobcat I will place my shot directly through its heart and lungs. It will die quickly and be easier to skin than a head shot cat.

A bobcat's anatomy is such that the carotid arteries lay close to the surface of the neck muscles, by applying pressure with the dispatch stick noose, the blood supply to the bobcats brain is shut off and results in almost intimidate disablement as the cat quickly loses consciousness and will die in less than one minute. This procedure is quick, painless for the bobcat and keeps the fur clean and blood free.

I always keep a bobcat that I am harvesting in the noose with the locking device engaged while I remake the set...I have never had one come back to life on me!

Big tom cat dispatched in less than a minute.

Because a bobcat is so susceptible to death in this manner it is imperative that if you are releasing a young bobcat or a female that you act quickly once the noose has been tightened and the cat is incapacitated. Quickly remove the trap while the tightened loop is locked in place. Then step back and release the lock and remove the noose from the cat's neck. You should be able to do this in less than 10 seconds once the bobcat has passed out. After you have released the cat, walk back 20 feet or so and wait for the cat to recover and slip away into the brush. You don't want a groggy confused bobcat jumping on you before it realizes it is free to run away!

After you have harvested a nice bobcat, remade your set, you can skin the cat near by or wait to do this in the comfort of your shed or barn. I can peel a freshly killed bobcat in less than 10 minutes, and one that has been dead for a few hours in 15 minutes or so.

Bobcat trapping season's are conducted during the cold winter months so under most conditions, waiting a few hours to skin a bobcat is no big deal. If the temperature is 40 degrees or above I would recommend you skin the cat immediately and put it in a cooler with ice to prevent the fur from slipping. Most states require a temporary possession tag for bobcats, and some require you take the skull or bottom jaw for age and DNA analysis, when you get permanent tags affixed, so don't forget to take care of this business at the same time.

Bobcats, like all predators have a very strong and active digestive system. The acid in their stomach must dissolve gristle, cartilage and bone, along with meat and some vegetable matter. When a bobcat is killed, its stomach lining begins to break down under the power of the acid it contains. It no longer has the ability to form a protective barrier that keeps a bobcat's stomach acid from leaching through its containment! In warm weather, animals that are not skinned quickly, the skin on their stomach will turn blue green and this can cause the fur to slip and make the pelt almost worthless. If you have seen green tinges on the stomach of a skinned predator you are seeing this acid reacting as it leaches through the animal. Because of this, if the weather is mild I make it a point to skin my catches right on the trap line. If the weather is near or below freezing, this is not a serious problem and skinning your catch at home in a warm garage or fur shed, at the end of the day is recommended.

During warm spells or in some areas of the country you may even need to carry a cooler with ice to put your skinned pelts in. Always keep skinned pelts dry and above the melting ice and water in the bottom of a cooler. I put my fur in a Ziploc bag and keep it in a plastic bin that sits on top the ice and water.

After you have dispatched a bobcat and are ready to skin the animal, I recommend you give it a shot of flea spray and put it in a garbage bag for a few minutes before skinning. Once the fleas are toes up, remove any burrs or dried dirt from the skin with a curry comb or dog brush.

Next, hang the cat from a wire, twine or skinning gambrel by one hind foot. (I recommend wearing nitrate or latex gloves while skinning any type of furbearer). Cut the hide around all four wrists, just going through the skin. Now grasp the hind leg that is not held with the wire, and stretch the leg so there is a somewhat straight line from the back edge of the back leg to the anus and the edge of the other back leg. Being careful to make a straight clean cut, use a sharp two or three inch scaple or skinning knife, and just cut through the skin from writs to just past the anus and then to the other wrist. Come back to the anus and cut around it without damaging the tail. Now carefully work the skin off the back legs by pulling and carefully using the knife to free the areas that stick.

Every trapper should have a tail stripper to pinch the tail bone and slide the hide off the tail. Once the tail is free the pelt can be pulled down toward the head and removed like a sock. Use the knife carefully and only cut the membrane that holds the skin to the muscles.

Around the front legs the hide can be a little tight and a phillips screwdriver works well once the arm pits are free you can put the screw driver through the opening left by the free skin and pull down with a hand on each end of the screwdriver. Carefully skin out to the circle cut around the wrists and slide the leg fur off over the paws.

Now pull the skin down to the neck and work it over the head. Care must be taken to leave the eyelids, ears, lips and nose on the skin as you skin out the head. If you have never skinned an animal before have and

Peeling a prime bobcat, is quick and easy

experienced trapper or taxidermist show you how it is done. Create good habits from the beginning and skinning will become easy for you.

If you are saving a pelt for a taxidermy mount, the paws and claws must be left on the fur and the foot, must be completely skinned out.

A couple of things that I do while skinning is use powdered borax to get a good grip on the hide. I sprinkle a little borax on the slick spots and you can get a good grip on things. Borax is a cleaning detergent found in the laundry department of most stores. It acts like an antimicrobial agent and is commonly used by taxidermists. It is harmless but the fine powder should not be inhaled. I dust the flesh side of my skins with borax before putting them on the stretcher to keep them from sticking to the stretcher and to destroy bacteria.

After skinning, a bobcat must be fleshed out on a fleshing beam with a curved fleshing knife. All the flesh and fat must be scraped off the hide, and the ear cartilage removed. The skin then must be placed on the stretcher skin side out for a few hours so that it dries on the surface and will not stick to the stretcher when the hide is put on fur side out. The skin should not be left so long with the skin side out, that it holds its shape, and is not pliable. It should not be difficult to turn and put back on the stretcher fur side out. In a dry climate three or four hours is fine. With higher relative humidity wait 6 hours. The process can be sped up with the use of a fan. If you use a fan you can turn your hides in an hour or two.

As I mentioned earlier, I use a little powdered borax on the skin to help the dried pelt slide off the stretcher when it is completely dry.

There are several ways to stretch or put up a bobcat pelt. The best and most up-to-date method is called the Nevada Stretch. This stretch exposes all of the underbelly fur from nose to tail and makes it easy for the fur buyer to see all of the markings and evaluate and grade the fur quickly.

To properly use this method you need some heavy duty push tacks and a wooden stretcher with a long center tail board and three bolts and nuts that can adjust for the width, length and the tail of the bobcat.

The center board, also acts as a flat surface to help tack out the back legs of the bobcat. The front legs are tacked up toward and parallel to the chin. The ears are tacked up toward the cheek ruffs. When done properly, the pelt will appear as a solid unit from the nose to the back legs on the belly side and all of the white fur will appear on the stomach side and the bobcats back fur on the back side of the stretcher.

Skinning and Fur Handling Tools

For skinning and taking care of bobcat fleshing and fur put-up there are many tools and tricks that make the job easier. Always wear hand protection such as neoprene gloves or tight fitting, coated painter gloves while skinning furbearers. Be prepared to quickly sterilize any cuts with rubbing alcohol and antibiotic ointment and a band-aid to prevent infection or contacting some blood born pathogen. Keep an eye on any wound and if it gets hot, inflamed or painful seek medical attention immediately. Though not common you can contact the plague, or rabies through contact

Beautifully stretched bobcats using The Nevada Stretch. Stock Photo

with blood and animal fluids.

Carefully choose a professional pelting knife for two reasons. They are designed for the job of skinning furbearers and they are very easy to sharpen. Do not use your pelting knife to cut through bones, remove bobcat jaws or anything other than just cut through the thin skin and membrane holding the pelt to the animal. For other heavy duty cutting tasks use a

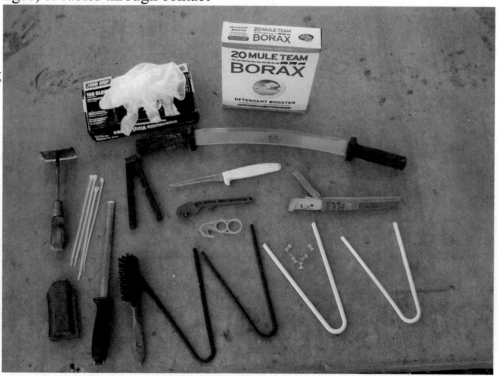

Fleshing knife, pelting knife, tail stripper and tail splitters, filet knife, Various sharpeners, fur brush, plastic coat hangers for drying front legs

60

beefy lock back pocket knife and some sharp side cutters.

A furberaer sized skinning gambrel is a nice tool that makes skinning more convenient. I like a steel gambrel with a foot of chain and small steel loop on each side that I can half hitch around an animals ankle.

Another indispensable tool is a tail splitter. This small pointed tool with a finger hole and a razor blade set in the hook works like a charm to split any tail for easy removal from the tail bone without damaging the fur.

As I mentioned earlier I also have a heavy duty lock-back pocket knife that I use for heavy cutting tasks of removing bobcat jaws or the occasional skinning out the feet of animals for the taxidermy trade. Cutting the claws free from the heavy ligaments that hold them to the bones of the feet and ankles will dull your thin bladed skinning knife.

A pair of sharp side cutters, used in the carpentry trade to nip nails and wire are great for removing bobcat jaws. Many states require the bottom jaw of bobcats to be submitted when you have them tagged with a permanent Cities transportation tag. This tag identifies the state the bobcat was trapped in and is a record that follows the bobcat all the way to the final purchaser. International treaty and laws protect many animal species from over harvest and poaching and the cities program helps maintain bobcat laws and regulations.

After a bobcat is skinned, the next chore is fleshing all the fat, flesh and cartilage off the pelt before putting it on the stretcher. To accomplish this task, a fleshing knife and fleshing beam is used. The best systems complement each other with the curvature of the beam closely matching that of the knife. This helps prevent cuts and tears in the skin while removing the flesh from the hide.

A heavy vinyl or leather apron will keep your clothes free from from blood, grease and dirt, and will provide a good purchase when you push against the hide pinched between your thigh and the beam.

Starting from the nose work all the flesh off the animal toward the tail. A fleshing knife is not very sharp, rather it is used to push the flesh down and off without cutting through the hide. Rotate the skin around the beam as you go down. As you work your way down the bobcat slide the nose end side of

61

the skin down between the beam and your thigh to keep a comfortable distance between the bobcat skin and your arms with the fleshing knife.

Carefully remove all flesh and fat from the hide and trim any bit of flesh from around the eyes, lips and ears. When you have a clean fleshed hide, examine the fur for blood or grease and clean it off with a damp rag, some dry borax or a handful of sawdust shavings.

Now the bobcat is ready for the initial stretch. This is done by putting the hide on the stretcher flesh side out for a few hours to allow the flesh to lose its sticky tack and dry enough that the remainder of the process can be finished with the fur side out.

As I mentioned a couple time earlier, I like to dust the fresh cleaned skin with a handful of borax before putting it on the stretcher. I rub the borax into the skin and remove any remaining grease with the dry borax.

Now, loosen the stretcher bolts and put the bobcat on the stretcher. Pull its back legs down firmly and put two tacks into the bottom of each back leg to hold it in place. Now widen the stretcher until it is 8 inches wide, and tighten the outside bolts. A very large bobcat may be stretched to 9 inches but bobcats are graded by size, fur primeness, color and markings. So we are going to stretch the bobcat to show each of these features to our fur buyer.

Next center the tail board and make sure that the board extends up to the base of the tail. Pull the tail down firmly and tack it out to its full width and length. Do the same for the fur from the bobcats rump. Tack it down flat across and firmly down.

On the belly side we are going to stretch the fur from the inside of the legs together and down firmly and tack it in five or six

This is fur in the initial stretch phase with some ready to turn.

places along each leg. Pull the leg hide as wide as it will go and tack it down each side and up to the hip.

Tack the lower jaw up. Now we are done with the tacks for a while. In the photos you will see some plastic coat hanger ends that have been cut off to about 10 inches. Squeeze one of these together and insert it in one leg and pull the leg tight. Do this to the other leg and then let the legs just hang out for now to start the drying process.

I usually give the hide 4 to 6 hours of dry time before turning the skin. The skin should kind of hold its shape but not be rigid. The flesh side should be dry to the touch but not hard or crinkly. If I am in a hurry to put up fur I will run a box fan on my drying hides. If you use a fan it will cut the drying time in half.

When the hide has lost its tack and is dry to the touch, it is time to turn the skin for the final stretch. Stretch the hide in the very same way as you did before but with the fur side out. The bobcat should be centered and symmetrical on the form. The fur colors should be balanced and all the white belly fur should be shown on the belly and the back fur on the back.

After your bobcat has started to dry for a few hours with the fur side out. You can pin up the ears with a couple push tacks to hide the inside of the ear and the front legs to show the white belly fur of the arm pits.

Within a week your fur should be dry and can be carefully taken off the stretcher. Remove all the tacks, and remove the bolts and nuts keeping the stretcher tight. Turn the bobcat upside down and tap the nose and tip of the stretcher on the ground gently a few times. The fur should slip off the stretcher. Examine the inside and make sure everything is dry and holds its form. If there are any spots not fully dry, rub in some borax and put the hide back on the stretcher loosely and snug the bolts back up. You probably won't have to put any tacks into the hide as it should hold its form. Leave the fur a few additional days and check it again. I live in a very low relative humility environment so I seldom have fur drying issues. Running a fan is the best way to dry fur in a more humid area.

Fur Sales and Fur Market

Selling your bobcat pelts to gain the most for your efforts takes some knowledge and understanding of the fur market. I suggest that every trapper subscribe to a good trapping magazine that has a fur market report section that can be monitored for the seasonal fluctuations in fur prices. World events and the currency of the major countries that purchase fur are determining factors in market demand and price. The major fur buying countries have been Russia and China with other eastern block countries. Saudi Arabia has been another strong purchaser of luxury goods. Cold winters and strong currency in these countries usually translates into good prices for the trapper.

There are three places that most trappers can sell their fur. They can locate a traveling country buyer that travels around and purchases fur. This is a very convenient way to sell your fur but my experience has shown that this method usually gets you the least return for your fur. This is a good way to make some expense money during the season by selling some lesser quality fur.

Fur Auction. I have sold a lot of fur at this auction over the years!

The second way to sell your fur is to a mail in fur clearing house. This too is a convenient way to sell and will usually yield more money for your fur than the country buyer. Most years however, the best way to maximize your fur profit is by taking your fur to a fur auction. Some state trappers associations hold yearly auctions for their members. Here your furs are divided into lots of like color, size and primeness. At an auction many international buyers will bid on your fur and the highest bidder will win the auction. There are a couple drawbacks and possible

Canada's Premier Supplier of Furbearer Management and Marketing Equipment

www.furharvesters.com

pitfalls to an auction. One drawback is that you have to pay a commission to the auction house where you sell your fur. It is usually small, but be aware of this and find out how much the auction will cost you. Another drawback is that you may not get your money right away. The auction house will usually mail you a check minus the commission fee. The final possible pitfall with all types of sales is that the market can swing from good to better or from good to bad without warning. I keep my finger on the pulse of the fur market all year and if the market is really good early, I will sell about half my fur to a mail house, and take my chance that the auction will be even better. If the market were to weaken just before the auction, I have already made some good money to cover my expenses. I may sell some of my remaining fur and then hold over some of my pelts for another year, or even watch and see if there is a late uptick in prices after the auctions are over. I have seen some strong late surges some years and I sure like being positioned to take advantage of these prices!

To hold fur over for a year can be risky. The market may weaken further or your fur could get damaged if not stored properly. I would not hold over fur longer than one year and only do this if you can store it properly. To be stored properly, it needs to be vacuum packed and frozen in a chest, deep freeze. You should probably have a deep freezer that is dedicated to this to prevent disputes with your wife or family! You should keep an eye on your fur and make sure everything is working on a regular basis. One year we had lightening strike a tree in our yard and knock out my fur freezer. I lost some valuable pelts before I discovered the problem with the freezer. I was not a happy camper!

Odds and Ends

In closing here I want to give a few tips and insights into dealing with trapline problems. Too many people in today's world have too much money and too much time on their hands. It is these seeds that will sprout people with a strong, albeit wrong opinion about trapping. They will not understand State game laws, wildlife management objectives, or give thought to the ways Nature manages her children if we do not step into the process. Nature is neither kind or painless with starvation, drought, overpopulation or disease. Man has been a natural part of the eco system for thousands of years. With the growth of modern populations, wildlife must be carefully managed to keep things in balance. Very few people realize that in areas without

trapping, wildlife agencies use aerial gunning, cyanide guns, and even poison to keep human populations protected from rabies, mange and predator depredation. If trappers don't help in the management, this amazing resource goes to waste.

Sometimes you will start to have trap line theft. This will either be from anti-trappers, or from other trappers and outdoorsmen stealing your valuable fur. This is a disheartening situation that can spiral out of control fast. The first thing you need to do is report this to local wildlife law enforcement as well as local sheriff's office. Then you need to do things to protect yourself from future theft.

Two things that you can do right away is to move your traps to another location, and add trapline security measures. You can adjust your trap anchoring system to make it hard for thieves to take your traps. Earth anchors can be employed without the use of quick links so thieves must dig up your traps to steal them. This does not protect your fur but it certainly helps protect your traps. You can do a better job of hiding traps or use drowning sets to hide catches. You can use one way slides and grapple drags to get furbearers out of sight and mind.

For the past 5 years I have started using trail cameras on my trapline in areas that are prone to theft problems. I try to put my cameras in areas where I can pick up license plate numbers as well as facial identification. Here again you must hide your cameras well and lock them up or, yep, you guessed it they will steal your cameras too!

You will be surprised at how well photos of a thief posted at the local sporting good store or on facebook will nip your problems in the bud!

Another potential problem that you may have in some areas are mountain lions, eating your bobcats out of the traps. It is pretty discouraging when a $500 bobcat is eaten out of a trap after you worked long and hard to catch one. This is a tough situation with only one solution, find some one with hounds and hunt some mountain lions!

Removing mountain lions from traps is tricky and down right dangerous. If you live close to a fish and wildlife office you can get someone to help you let the lion out. I have a long, stout catch release pole that I can choke lions down and take the trap off by myself, but it can be nerve racking.   Mountain lion left this at one of one of my bobcat traps.

Getting ready to release a trapped lion...not for the faint of heart!

Make sure the lion is firmly caught and anchored before approaching it. Once you get the noose around its neck, clamp down hard and keep it tight until the lion passes out. Keep the choke lock on while you monitor the big cat for a few more seconds. Now work fast and get the trap off. Just leave the trap there, take the noose off the lion and get back at least 30 feet and out of sight. Wait and watch until the mountain lion comes to its senses and wanders away. When the lion is safely gone, you can go examine your trap. I usually will pull my trap once it has caught a lion. Bobcat traps are not designed to take the abuse of a lion and your trap will most likely be out of whack and will need some adjustment before redeployment.

In closing, I will give you a final thought. The last few years, I have been using Google Earth with good success to locate pinch points, rock formations, water crossings and many other features that can help with laying out and planning potential new trap lines. Remember no work in the office can overcome the need for actual scouting and work in the field looking for sign and verifying your theories or hunches.

Good luck to you in your bobcat trapping efforts!

Fur Primeness Chart

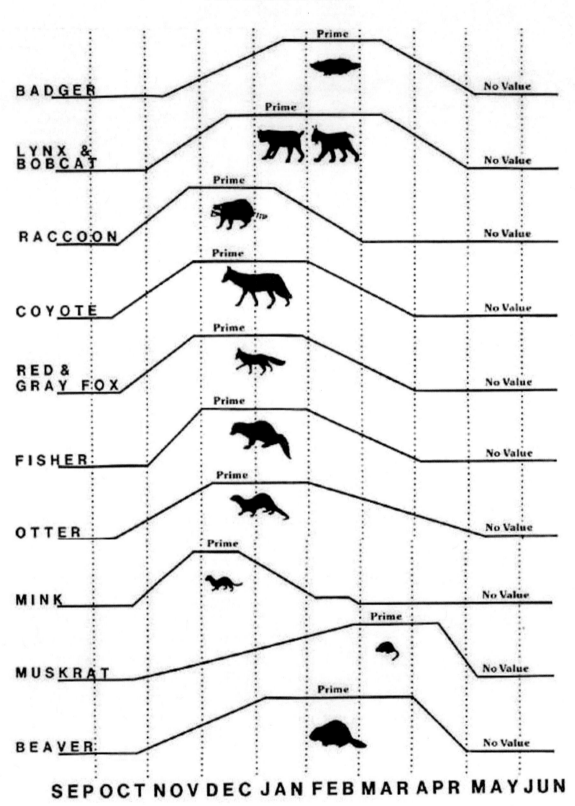

Trap Diagram

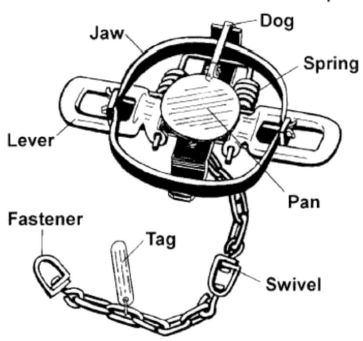

Parts of the Foothold Trap

Lynx & Bobcat - Cased fur out, front legs in, lower lip off, ear cartilage out.

Lynx and bobcat are valuable furbearers which can realize a very good value for the fur harvester when properly handled.

Great care should be taken right in the field to ensure the skins are going to receive their full potential price. Use the best harvesting tools possible and check your traps often. Damage caused by improperly set snares or allowing the cat to freeze to the ground can lower the price. Care should be used by placing your catch in a clean burlap bag right in the field and by pelting the animal as quickly as possible. Before skinning the cat, ensure that it is clean and dry, comb the cat completely to remove any dirt or blood. The use of clean dry sawdust will help in cleaning the fur of any mud or dirt.

Cats are cased skinned. Start at one hind leg and cut across to the other leg on the belly side of the anus. Pull the pelt away from the flesh with your fingers, until you have exposed the flesh around the tail bone and belly. Use your tail stripper to remove the short tail bone. Split the tail. Peel the pelt down to the front legs and skin them out. Next, skin down to the ears and eyes, finishing off with trimming the nose cartilage close to the hide. Remove the lower lip. Board pelt after removing any excess fat or grease. Remember to sew any bullet holes or tears at this stage. Using mink boards, pin the front legs to dry. Allow about 24 hours for the pelt to dry then turn the pelt fur out and place back on the board until dry. You can pin the ears flat to the head. Once the pelt is dry, give the skin a good combing with a slicker style brush. We recommend one size board for both lynx and bobcat.

Lynx & Bobcat Board Size
Board Length = 72 inches

2" = 3"
6" = 4 5/8"
12" = 5 1/4"
24" = 6 3/8"
72" = 8"

Lynx Pelt Size

1X	Over 39"	Over 99cm
LG	35" - 39"	89-99cm
LM	34" - 35"	86-89cm
MD	31" - 34"	78-86cm
SM	Under 31"	Under 78cm

Bobcat Pelt Size

3X	Over 44"	Over 112cm
2X	40" - 44"	102-112cm
1X	36" - 40"	91-102cm
LG	32" - 36"	81-91cm
MD	28" - 32"	71-81cm
SM	Under 28"	Under 71cm

Nevada Style Stretchers with tail board. I use a screw gun and wood screws to adjust the width and height. You can also drill holes and use bolts and wing nut screws to adjust them. I have over 200 stretchers and sometimes every one is full. Using a screw gun is much faster!

On the following page is a Nevada Stretch style stretcher. If you want to make some of these stretchers, print the pattern on your printer then use the dimensions to cut some stretchers from 3 inch pine boards. I like to put a slight bevel on the edge of the stretchers with a router. A piece of leather strip or rubber strip from an inner tube stapled at the top works well to keep the tops together.

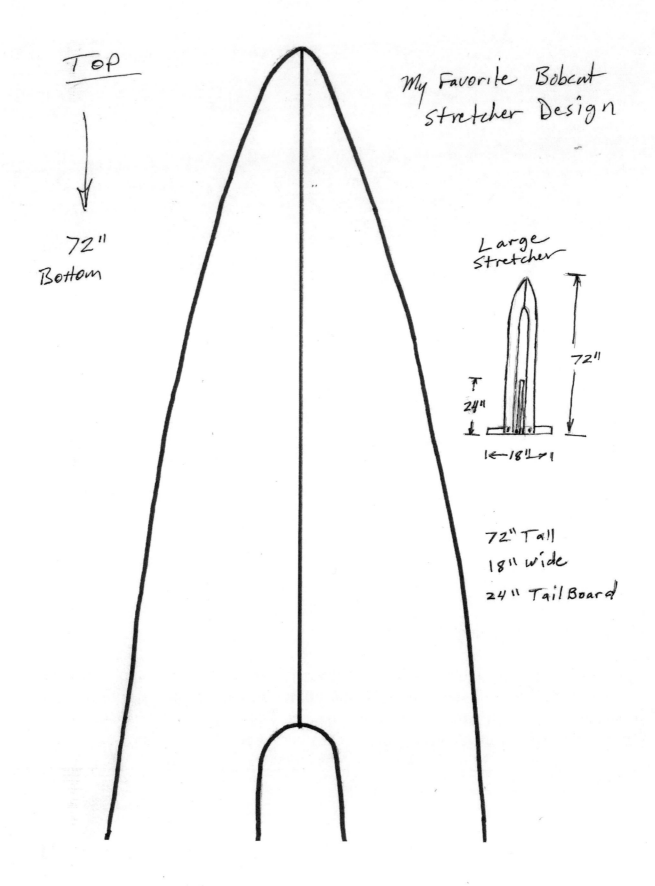

Top

72"
Bottom

My Favorite Bobcat
Stretcher Design

Large
Stretcher

72"

24"

|←—18"—→|

72" Tall
18" wide
24" Tail Board

72

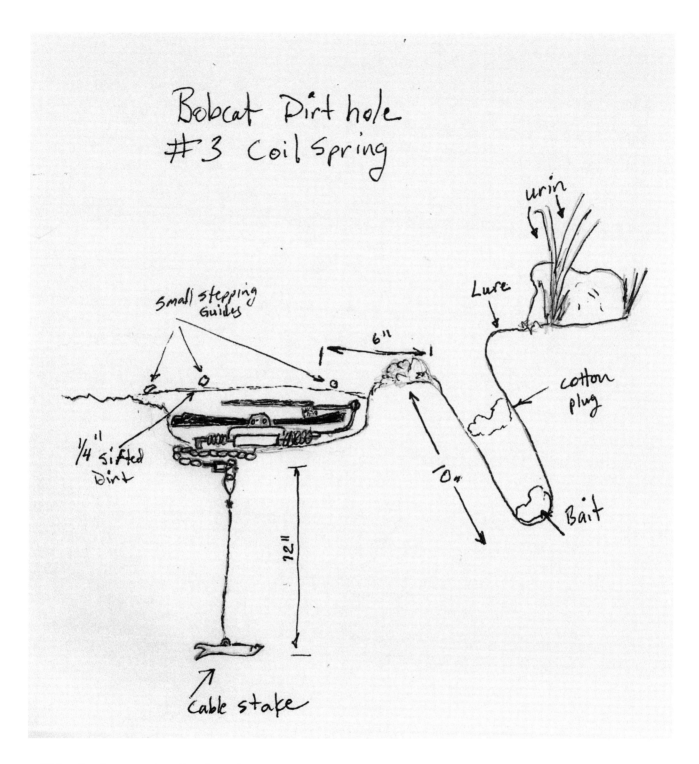

Dirt hole set detail, showing correct depths and distances for bobcat trap sets.

Double dirt hole set: Trap is between holes 6" out. Bobcat caught in set

Walk through set:

Here I used a graple drag because the bed rock was 6 inches down.
Nice prime gray fox. We catch a lot of gray's in our bobcat sets.

Flat Set:

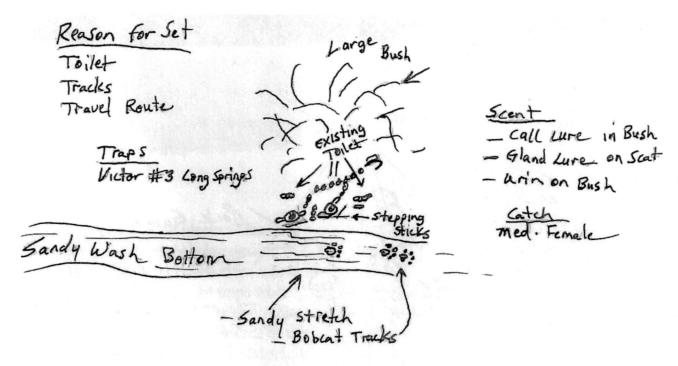

Reason for Set
Toilet
Tracks
Travel Route

Traps
Victor #3 Long Springs

Large Bush

Existing Toilet

stepping Sticks

Sandy Wash Bottom

— Sandy stretch
— Bobcat Tracks

Scent
— Call Lure in Bush
— Gland Lure on Scat
— Urin on Bush

Catch
Med. Female

76

Trail Along Cut Bank

Cut Bank

Trail

Bottom of Wash or Cut

Possible other Trap Location

Look for Sign Tracks, Trail

Staging Sticks

Rock Guides

2 #3 coils

Rock Guides

Log Guide

Bobcat Toilet urine, Gland Lure Added

Cats path

Cats path

Dirt Hole

Buried Bait

Possible 3rd Set

#2 Coil Staked 8" From Hole, urine & Gland Lure only

Cats path

Prevailing Wind

— Set where Trail Narrows

— Traps 16" Apart
— Bait Buried Between Traps
— pathway Left Beside Bait
— Natural or Created Toilet

77

Old Whiskey Bottle Set

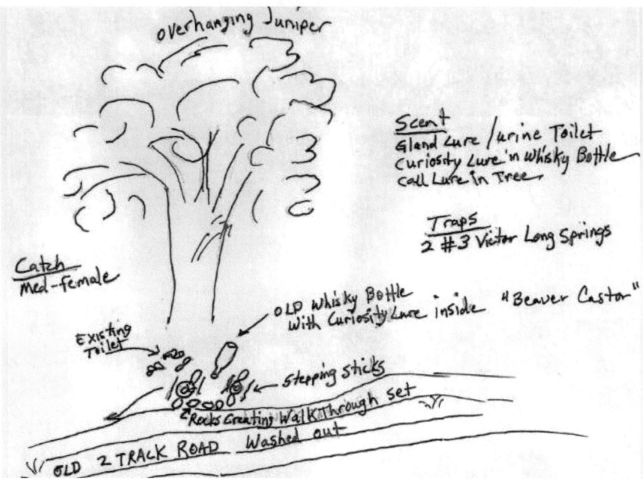

This set was made along an old unused 2 track road near a lake. Bobcat tracks were coming and going. I caught medium female first and let her go. 4 days later I caught a nice tom. Later I caught two coyotes at this same set before I pulled the trap. Any trap set that pulls in a $400 tom bobcat and two $50 coyotes is ok in my book!

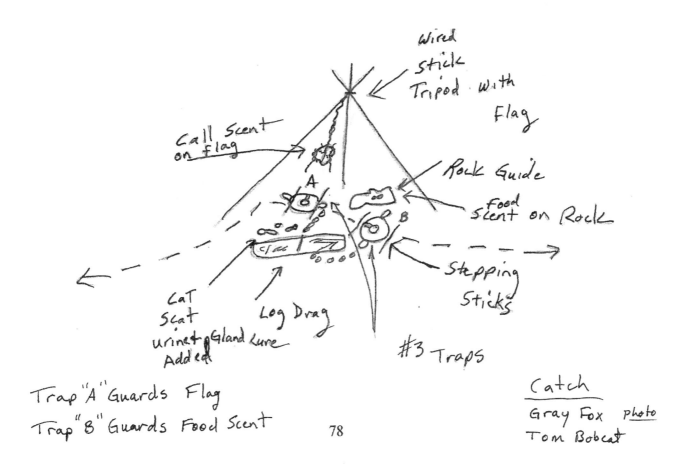

Wired
stick
Tripod with
Flag

Call Scent
on flag

Rock Guide

Food
Scent on Rock

A

B

Stepping
Sticks

CaT
Scat
urine + Gland Lure
Added

Log Drag

#3 Traps

Trap "A" Guards Flag
Trap "B" Guards Food Scent

78

Catch
Gray Fox   Photo
Tom Bobcat

I anchored my trap directly at the set and the bobcat destroyed it
If I would have used a drag the set would have been left intact

79

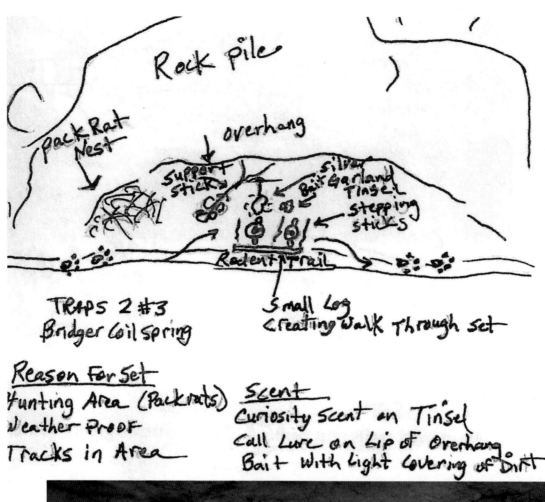

Rock pile

pack Rat Nest

overhang

support sticks

silver Garland Tinsel
Bait

stepping sticks

Rodent Trail

TRAPS 2 #3
Bridger Coil spring

Small Log
creating Walk Through set

<u>Reason For Set</u>
Hunting Area (Packrats)
Weather Proof
Tracks in Area

<u>Scent</u>
Curiosity scent on Tinsel
Call Lure on Lip of Overhang
Bait With light Covering of Dirt

We have a lot more gray fox than red's but I catch quite a few fox in my bobcat sets especially when the weather gets cold and they are tempted by bait or lure!

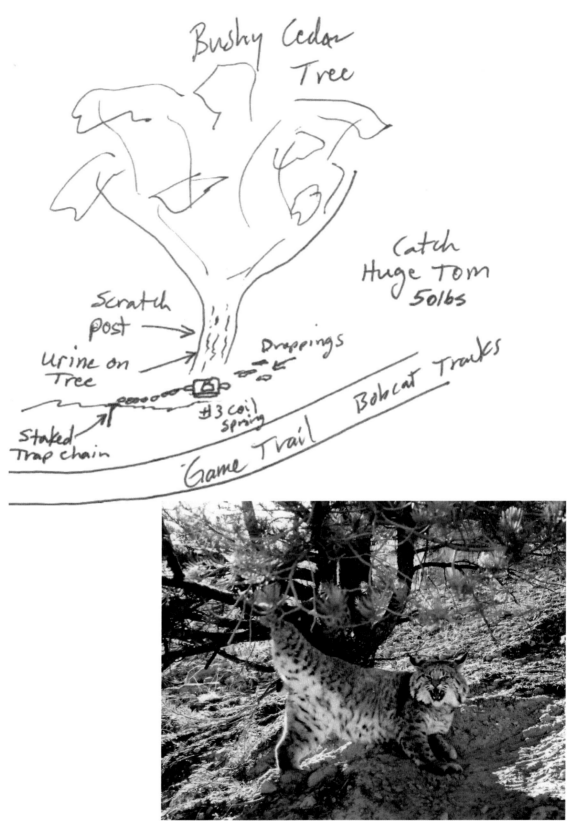

Bushy Cedar Tree

Catch
Huge Tom
50lbs

Scratch Post →

Urine on Tree →

Droppings

#3 coil spring

Staked Trap chain →

Game Trail

Bobcat Tracks

This huge tom bobcat is the best I have ever caught at 50lbs he is a monster!

Bait and Lure for Bobcat Sets

Bobcats are very visual hunters. They have a well developed sense of smell and hearing, by appealing to all these senses with your sets you have a great chance of catching any bobcat that comes along. Two key factors are evident that will increase your chance of attracting and catching bobcats in your trapping sets. 1- Your traps need to be right along the path of a bobcat's travel route. 2- Your attractions need to be custom tailored for bobcats. To do this follow these guidelines.

Set your bobcat traps on sign. If you find bobcat tracks, droppings, scratch up marks on trees and the ground, you can be sure you are on a good bobcat location.

Use enticing bobcat baits to get the best response from them at your bobcat sets. Bobcats like the smell of fish, chicken and rabbit. By using fresh bait from these animals in your dirt hole sets, you will excite their response to get the bait.

The best scents to use at bobcat sets are bobcat gland lure, beaver castor lure, and long distance call lure with skunk musk. In fact I use each of these scents at most of my bobcat sets. Gland lure is applied against any backing and a shot of bobcat urine is made to the same location. I usually apply beaver castor to a 12" long slim stick that is stuck into the ground toward the back of the set. A bobcat investigating the set will have the tenancy to smell and rub on this stick. They love the smell of beaver castor. I use long distance call lure above my trap to not only appeal to their curiosity but increase the chance of smelling the set if they are not traveling exactly on the location I have chosen. Skunk musk can be carried quite a ways and the smell appeals to bobcats.

In cold weather it is a good idea to put a very small amount of your long distance call lure right at the set, in the dirt hole or against your backing such as a cow skull. Cold weather cuts down all animals ability to smell a scent and bobcats coming into skunk smells may lose interest in the set if they cannot locate the source when they get close to a set. For this reason it can be a good idea to put a little of your call lure directly at the set.

Bobcats are very visual animals. They do most of their hunting by eyesight. Fluttering flags above your sets are very appealing to their hunting instinct. Some of my favorite flags are bird wings, fake fur, white rags or cotton batting and Christmas tree garland. In some areas, bird wings are not allowed. At any rate the best flags are made of contrasting material. If your soil and terrain is light brown-green, use white or black flags. If there is snow-covered landscape, use dark brown or black flags.

The best flags flutter and move with the slightest breeze. For this reason I like to use a fishing swivel on heavy fishing line to hang my flags. I like my flags to be about 4 feet off the ground. This is elevated enough that they can be above ground vegetation, yet still low enough to catch a bobcats eye. I want a bobcat to feel like it can get to the flag without doing weird things like climbing and jumping. If a bobcat must pass over your traps to investigate the flag,

Christmas tree garland flag used as an attration above a cave set.

there is a much greater likelihood of a catch. It is often on these flags that I place my long distance call lures.

  There are two set types I use limited scent and zero bait. The first set is a walk-through set. Just like a trail set, a walk-through is designed to catch a cat as it walks through the set. Because of this it must be right on a bobcat trail. I do not want to stop a bobcat as it walks through the set. I want the cat in motion and stepping on the places I have left for him to step. One spot is right on the trap pan. Save your sent for dirt holes, flat and flagged sets.The other set I do not use bait or curiosity lures is the toilet set. At the toilet set I only use bobcat gland lure and bobcat urine.   I want bobcats focused on territorial instinct at a toilet set. They are there investigating their territory and the best response here is appealing to this instinct. Blend in the set and use a drag or slide system to keep a trapped bobcat from destroying the area. In the past there have been some interesting inventions of squeakers and sound makers to use in conjunction to trapping, particularly bobcat trapping. I have used several different brands of squeakers and sound makers and my consensus is that they do work, but the extra cost and effort as well as the possibility as attracting the attention of hunters, hikers and campers in the field, do not warrant the addition of them to your arsenal.

If you have some remote areas to trap and want to experiment by all means try them out. I will warn you though, that you must have the sound makers behind the set and not up in a tree, or the bobcat will ignore the set and climb the tree. After the cat has jerked the battery bunny down, it will either lose interest in the whole situation or take off with your noise maker.

Nice bobcat taken at a pack rat nest set up under the edge of a big rock
Gland lure and urine were used up at the edge of the rock X Trap was at <O>
Long distance call lure used on the top edge of the rock. L

I have had better luck with small wind chimes above my sets for bobcats, that electronic calls, but a part of my focus in trapping is not just bobcats. My goal is to pay my bills, make money and catch any valuable fur bearing animal....so I keep all my sets friendly to coyotes and fox and offer back up sets to all my bobcat sets. A wind chime will almost certainly guarantee that no coyote or red fox will work a set anywhere within hearing distance of a wind chime.

I am not going to suggest any particular brand of scent or lure, but I would stick with the better know lure manufacturers that have been around successfully for years. Then experiment each season with new lures. A key point to understand is that not all lures and scents will work equally well in the many different areas of the country. You must find what works well for bobcats and predators in your neck of the woods.

Various brands of bobcat scent & bait by some major lure and bait manufacturers
Stock Photo

Remember no lure or scent can take the place of correct trap location. No lure will bring in bobcats that do not exist in the area you are trapping. Trap on location and focus on making your sets appealing to bobcats interests of food, sex, curiosity, and competition with other bobcats and predators and you will trap the elusive bobcat.

The end...of the tail.

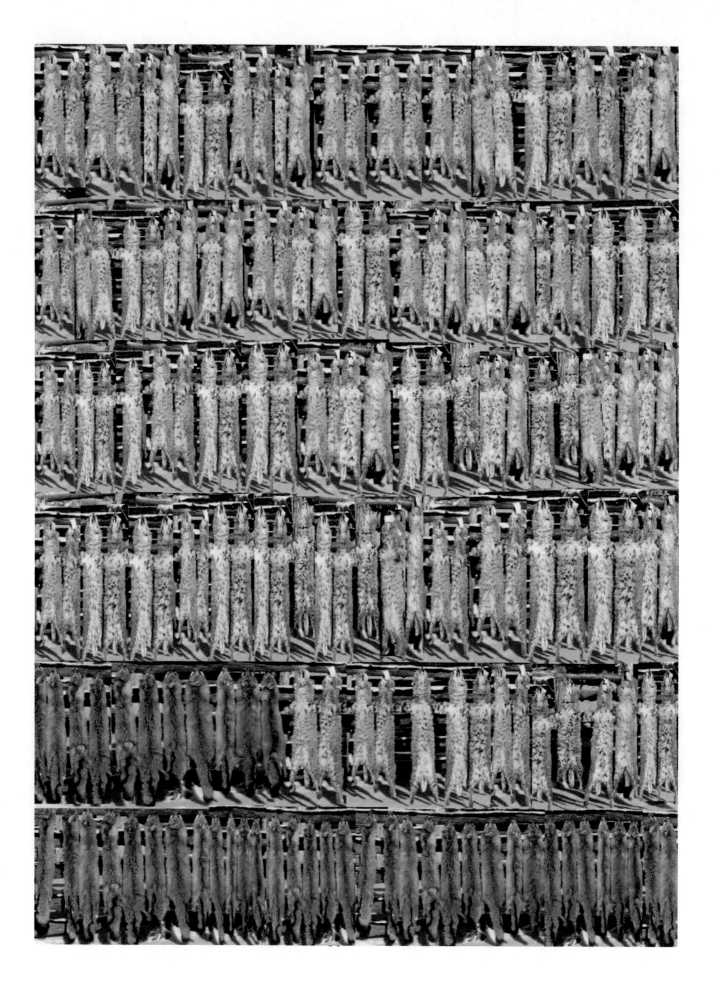

Made in the USA
Las Vegas, NV
10 November 2020

10688512R00052